Praise for
Scream and Run Naked

"Dr. Alison Arnold has been working with my elite athletes for over 10 years and has based her teachings on the truths that she shares in *Scream and Run Naked*. She and her lessons have been like an assistant coach encouraging us daily to maximize our unique abilities and to shine bright in our sport. This book will help you become all that you were created to be. Many thanks for assisting so many gymnasts to find their dreams and go after them."
—*Mary Lee Tracy, Coach of 1996 Gold Medal Winning USA Gymnastics Team*

"*Scream and Run Naked* is simply inspiring. Never have I been so motivated, moved and gently guided. This book is so relevant and encompassing that I found I could open to any page and be touch, moved and inspired."
—*James Keenley, Radio Talk Show Host and TV Producer*

"This insightful, inspirational, healing book is your *Wake-up Call!* It can guide us on the quest for happiness, self discovery, and self awareness. I hope everyone benefits from it as I have."
—*Kitty Carruthers Conrad, Olympic Silver Medalist 1984 Pairs Figure Skating*

"This is a book of wonders. Some of the most heartfelt and headiest teachings I've encountered in one amazingly digestible, personal and warm volume. I recommend it without reservation. Although the book is a chronological tale, it can be opened anywhere, started anywhere and stopped anywhere, and deliver immediate value, perspective and energy. Use this book for reflection, for sharing, and for the times when things seem the most helpless and beyond control."
—*Stan Slap, International Speaker, Author, and Business Consultant; President, Slap*

"*Scream and Run Naked* is an irresistible invitation. Dr. Alison Arnold understands the science of achievement, yet she will lead you far beyond mere achievement. Her amazing book shares the ancient secrets, the modern truths and the practical day-to-day steps for creating an extraordinary life... the one you have dared to only dream. This is a book for us all – business people, athletes, actors, and monks!"
—*Jim Manton, President, Manton Advisory Services, Inc.*

"This book is thought provoking and stopped me in my hustle world to evaluate my life passions. It encourages the reader to evaluate and prioritize life'
—*Michael G. Vica*

D1512158

Also by Alison Arnold:

Scream & Run Naked

Lessons from a Neurotic's Journey to Nepal

by Alison Arnold
with Michele St. George

Head Games Press

Copyright © 2006 Alison Arnold, Ph.D.

Published by Head Games, LLC
1830 N. Dayton Street, Phoenix AZ 85006
http://www.headgames.ws
http://www.screamandrunnaked.com

Printed in the United States of America
First Edition
April 2006
10 9 8 7 6 5 4 3 2 1

Publisher's Cataloging-in-Publication
Arnold, Alison
    Scream and Run Naked/Alison Arnold with Michele St. George
    — 1st ed.
    P.cm.
    ISBN: 0-9771434-0-6
    1. Spiritual Life 2. Self-actualization (Psychology)
    3. Arnold, Alison   I. Title

To all seekers with the courage to wake up
and Scream and Run Naked.
We do it together.

For the Source of all that is that I Am. May
this book help us remember our true
nature.

Contents

Acknowledgements

There are so many beautiful souls that have impacted this book.

Thank you Michele St. George for holding my hand, molding my words, and carrying me through this process. You took my jumbled words and stories and created something beautiful. Thank you for transforming this book. It never could have happened without your vision, belief, commitment, and patience!

Further credit goes to Patricia Turpin for brushing over this book with her quick wit, creativity, and unique flare. You helped give it just what it needed. And thank you to Ruth Suli-Urman for her final polishing and ongoing belief in this project.

I'm indebted to my friend and former business partner, Chris Dorris, who didn't scoff at my desire to depart for several months for spiritual practice. Instead he supported and encouraged me by saying "OK, partner, let's make it happen!"

I owe a tremendous debt of gratitude to my teachers in Nepal and Thailand for their guidance, kindness, and wisdom: Tsognyi Rinpoche, Younge Khachab Rinpoche, Khenpo Karten, Karme Dempchu, Giri Sedhain, Kelsang Rinpoche, Chokyi Nyma Rinpoche, Ajahn Amaro, and Tan Sumedo, among so many others.

Thank you to four of my mentors who have pushed me to give my gifts (albeit at times kicking and screaming): Bob Mosby, Steve Hardison, Jim Manton, and Mack Newton. You have always held the vision never allowing me to "play small."

A bow of gratitude to USA Gymnastics—you are the first people to love my work, believe in it, and give me a stage to stand upon. Thank you to Roe Kreutzer for changing my life every step of the way since age 6, to Kathy Kelly, and Mary Lee Tracy. It marked the beginning of a beautiful journey.

Thank you to my family. You have always loved and supported me in all of my crazy adventures.

Special Thanks for my workshop co-creator and co-facilitator, Jan Casalena. It has always been an honor to work with you and beside you. And to the staff, and hundreds of graduates of our workshop. Never have I've been so blessed as when I see you shine.

To my amazing tribe of friends. You are my greatest teachers. You have always believed in me when I had difficulty finding belief in myself. You raise me up.

The City of Saba

There is a glut of wealth in the city of Saba.
Everyone has more than enough.
Even the bath stokers wear gold belts.

Huge grape clusters hang down on every street
and brush the faces of the citizens.

No one has to do *anything*.

You can balance a basket on your head and walk
through an orchard, and it will fill by itself with
overripe fruit dropping into it.

Stray dogs stray in lanes full of thrown-out scraps
with barely a notice.

The lean desert wolf gets indigestion
from the rich food.
Everyone is fat and satiated with all the extra.

There are no robbers.
There is no energy for crime, or for gratitude,
and no one wonders about the unseen world.

The people of Saba feel bored with just the mention
of prophecy. They have no desire of any kind.

Maybe some idle curiosity about miracles, but that's it.

This over richness is a subtle disease.
Those who have it are blind to what's wrong and
deaf to anyone who points it out.

The city of Saba cannot be understood
from within itself:
But there is a cure, an individual medicine,
Not a social remedy:
Sit quietly, and listen for a voice within that will say,

Be more silent.

As that happens, your soul starts to revive.
Give up talking and your positions of power.
Give up the excessive money.
Turn toward teachers and prophets
who don't live in Saba.

They can help you grow sweet again
and fragrant
and wild and fresh
and thankful for any small event.

Jelaluddin Rumi
(translated by Coleman Barks)

Dying to Live

Journal entry 8/15/2001

"I am going to Nepal to learn how to die."

That cheerful thought abruptly popped me out of my morning meditation. Lovely. I was already a little nervous about this trip. Never one to give up, I took several deep, calming breaths, closed my eyes again, and immediately became aware of another question moving among the rising and falling thoughts of my chattering mind:

"Have I learned yet how to live?"

Are you afraid of dying? Even more tragic, are you afraid of living?

It is easy to flounder along in a never-ending pursuit of happiness, seized by what the poet David Whyte calls "unnamed longings." Do you have a feeling in your gut that there is something more to life that you are missing? Perhaps you long for fire and passion to fill your life or ache to grasp and fulfill your heart's desires. Do you crave a destiny of your own? In short, do you want to be fully *alive*? What is stopping you?

From the moment you came into this world, you have been heading steadily toward death. I know, it's grim, but the second you took your first breath, it became inevitable that you would someday take your last. The question is, what will you do in-between?

I attended the birthday party of an eighty-year-old woman, and her son showed a video he had made from the photos and home movies of her life. First I saw her as a baby in her parent's arms, then as a chubby toddler riding a tricycle, then as a young graduate, a bride, a young mother holding her own first born. Tears flowed down my cheeks as I watched scenes from her life. I wondered, "How quick did it all pass for her? Did she have any unfulfilled dreams? How quick will my life pass?" How quickly will yours?

Beyond your physical existence, beyond your body's needs and cravings, beyond your possessions, beyond even your hopes, fears, and desires, lies what the poet T.S. Eliot called "the still point":

Where past and future are gathered.
Neither movement from nor towards,
Neither ascent nor decline. Except for the point, the still point,
There would be no dance, and there is only the dance.

The still point is the moment in which you experience timelessness, with no thought of future or past. This is where the action of your life—the dance—takes place. You undoubtedly experience still points in your life, whether you recognize them or not. Still points are moments of being intensely aware of the present with no thoughts of regret or wistfulness about the past, no thoughts of worry or anticipation about the future, nothing but keen focus on what you are doing at the moment. Think of the best meal you have ever savored, your first romantic kiss, the hour your child was born, or the day your parent died. These are stillpoints: moments of time when your mind is focused and fully engaged in what you are doing; moments of time that fully capture your attention, engage you passionately, slowing the pace of your life; moments that you live.

Children tend to live at the still point because every moment is new, and everything is a source of wonder. Children set out to wildly and freely experience the mysterious and inviting world without concern for what others think. But soon parents and society grab those uncivilized little creatures by the scruff of the neck and say things like, "You can't run naked in the backyard; what will the neighbors think?" "You can't play in the rain, you'll catch a cold." "You can't wear those clothes, people will think you look strange." The message is, "If you don't behave the way we think you should, you may not be loved."

And so you mature, gradually confining your wondrous spirit, taming your unique self, and stifling your joy. Congratula -tions! You are now an acceptable and productive member of society. Coincidentally, you've also begun the slow decline towards death. "Childhood is the world of miracle and wonder," wrote playwright Eugene Ionesco, "As if creation rose, bathed in the light, out of the darkness, utterly new and fresh and astonishing. The end of childhood is when things cease to astonish us." Likewise, Albert Einstein declared that those who "can no longer pause to wonder and stand rapt in awe" are as good as dead already.

It's also far more difficult to be in the still point, to experience wonder and passion, when you live in the western world with its many demands and distractions. The Sufi poet Rumi wrote a poem over seven centuries ago about a mythical place called Saba. In it he writes about how people in Saba suffer from the subtle disease of having more than enough. As in Saba, life is fat and satiated with all the extras—a thousand toys, a thousand entertainments for those rare moments when we don't have anything else to do. No one wonders about the unseen world in a society where discussing the idea of God or Divinity is as dangerous as discussing politics or sex. How do you live, as Rumi suggests, a life that is wild and fresh and thankful in such a place?

Saba is an illusion; a dream in which you grow fat and content with whatever drifts your way, whatever your next paycheck will buy.

When I was in college, I gradually became aware that I was beginning to "flatline" my own life. Compelled to tout my importance and fit in socially, I'd tell others about my athletic accomplishments, my fascinating and worthwhile work in psychology, or the deep, meaningful spiritual retreat I had just attended, and all to convince them how "cool" I was. And yet, day in and day out, a monotone hum permeated my activities. I woke up, went for a run or to aerobics, went to my classes, attended academic meetings, changed for work, waited tables at a fancy Italian restaurant, came home, studied, and fell into bed. And, like a good citizen of Saba, whenever I felt empty or wrung out, I diverted my attention by going to see a movie, or buying myself new, soft-as-butter leather shoes, eating a pint of chocolate chip ice cream, or having a steamy affair. My narrow life consisted of my work, my body, my needs, my ideas, my drama, my things, my attractiveness, my way. And, despite all of this "myness," my life was not mine at all. I was living it, and talking it up, in a way calculated to please others. And I was filling it with meaningless amusements. My life was in no way self-determined, but created in unconscious patterns to please and gain the approval of others.

I confided my struggle to one of my favorite professors at my college, in Oregon. I saw him regularly for "supervision" meetings. He was a mustached hippie with red hair, keen blue eyes, and a renegade spirit. After we finished discussing my classes, there was a brief pause while I got up the courage to ask, "Do you ever feel more dead than alive? All I hear is the dull day-in-day-out hum of the machine in my head. What do you do to feel something? To feel alive?"

A rueful smile crossed his lips, he chuckled knowingly, and said, "Sometimes, on my property in the forest, no matter how hot, cold, or rainy, it is, I take off all of my clothes, and I run. I run through the trees as fast as I can, and I scream at the top of my lungs. I scream, I cry, I yell at God and the world. Sometimes I just drop to my knees, throw my head back, and wail to the sky." He leaned forward and looked me in the eyes,

" I dare life to seize me, to use me, to show me something more."

I was somewhat taken aback. I'm sure my eyes were wide with astonishment. I thought about asking him, "So, short of running naked in the forest, do you have any other suggestions?" But I didn't, I laughed. And he did, too. I knew that what he was saying was true. Sometimes you have to take off your armor. You have to face the world in naked vulnerability. Feel the cold. Embrace the wind. Dig your toes into the earth. And scream. Yell at the top of your lungs, "This is who I am!" But just how this earnest, society-pleasing, fun-loving girl from Arizona was going to do that, I didn't quite know.

The psychologist Carl Jung observed that we can't cure our unhealthy fears and obsessions—we can only outgrow them. This usually requires a spiritual awakening of some kind, he believed, and so I began to immerse myself in Buddhist and Eastern philosophy. Buddhism, particularly as it is practiced in the West, is more of a non-sectarian philosophy than a religion. Christians, Jews, Muslims, agnostics or atheists can incorporate Buddhist practices into their lives while remaining completely true to their own beliefs. At the core of Buddha's teachings is that we must "wake up" from our sleepwalking lives if we ever want to realize our true Self, and be able to see the true Self in others. We must wake up from the belief systems clouding our vision and really see the world for what it is.

The term "Buddha" actually means "One who is awake." The Buddha never claimed to be a god or a prophet, or even a saint, just a human being who learned to wake up. Buddhism is mostly free of any dogmatic beliefs, because Buddha simply didn't provide answers about the nature of God or an afterlife. Only one question is important in Buddhism: How are you living your life now?

Many centuries ago, Buddha taught that we are not separate from Creation, rather we are completely interconnected and interdependent with everything that is. The study of quantum physics, which teaches us about the nature of reality, has convinced many contemporary scientists that Buddha was right. "Quantum theory reveals a basic oneness of the universe," writes Fritjof Capra in *The Tao of Physics*. "It shows that we cannot decompose the world into independently existing smallest units. As we penetrate into matter, nature does not show us any isolated 'basic building blocks,' but rather appears as a complicated web of relations between the various parts of the whole."

Buddha warned that we suffer because we insist on standing apart from our wholeness, our Oneness, and we become attached to pieces of the whole. Many people misunderstand the concepts of non-attachment and desire in Buddhism, thinking that it means you must become ascetic or forsake all physical pleasures. Yet nothing is judged as "bad" in Buddha's philosophy. Money isn't bad, possessions aren't bad, electricity isn't bad, sex isn't bad, people aren't bad. These things are all a part of the whole. It's when we become obsessively attached to one fragment—my money, my beauty, my toys, my desires— that the suffering begins—and we begin to die inside.

Waking up is no guarantee against pain and the stresses and realities of the world. Jobs will still be lost, loved ones will die, diseases will occur. Sylvia Boorstein paraphrased one of Buddha's teachings beautifully:

"Pain is inevitable. Suffering is optional."

Buddhist practices are not an anesthetic against pain. Our very resistance to pain and insistence that we are special and should not have to endure any pain—the feeling of victimization, the "why me?"— is what creates suffering. We suffer when we insist that life be as we want it to be and refuse to surrender to what it is. Suffering is optional.

There is a Buddhist folktale about a woman who comes to the Buddha to ask that her suffering be taken away, for her child has just died. Buddha says to her, "I will take your suffering away; but first I want you to go through the village and ask until you find someone who has never lost a loved one."

The woman left at once, but at every house she visited, she heard stories of loss—a parent, a child, a friend, an uncle or an aunt. To be sure, there was joy and celebration as well, but she could not find a single house that had never known grief. As she heard the stories of the people, she began to understand her own story and her own loss. She returned to the Buddha no longer expecting miracles, at last able accept the loss, bury her child, and turn to others in compassion. "Thank you," she says to the Buddha.

Pain is also, like everything else in life, fleeting. As anyone who has come through a painful illness or loss will tell you, it increases your capacity for joy. "The deeper that sorrow carves into your being the more joy you can contain," writes the poet Kahlil Gibran. Pain also teaches us compassion, for we all experience anguish and grief.

Enlightenment will not look the same in you, or me, or your spouse, or your friend. We are living our own unique lives with our own unique purposes for being here. For me, enlightenment is a seduction, and a process. Don't we always feel most alive when we are in love? Life is the ultimate Lover. I want to devour every moment, every event, and every person that life sends my way.

Think of how you take in a new lover, how you seduce him or her with your rapt attention. You study the curve of his jaw, the curl of her lashes, the strength of his hands, the flecks of gold in her eyes, melting in the warmth of such intimate awareness. I once sat at dinner with a new love and was not even able to swallow because I was so mesmerized by the way he buttered a piece of bread. He was the most beautiful bread butterer I had ever seen! That's how I want to take in life.

Spiritual practices and ideas are teaching me to be awake, aware, and, most of all, free to seduce my life with wild joy and abandon.

A Pilgrimage

Studying Buddhism helped me overcome the feeling of being "the ghost in the machine" in my life. But, still, I wanted more. Going to Nepal to immerse myself in spiritual study and practice first became a goal for me in 1990, but I was "too busy" to get there right away. Ten years later, I still had not gone. I had established my psychology practice, and I frequently found myself in conversations with people who were searching for more passion and awareness in their lives. One day at a conference, I asked the participants what they would do if they only had a year to live. Ask yourself that question—

it's a wonderful way to focus the mind on what is truly important to you. When I answered the question for myself I realized that if I were to die that day, the only thing I would really regret was not going to Nepal. It took me a year to plan for a fifteen-week stay in Nepal as well as a monastery in Thailand. Departure was set for September 2001.

I left for Nepal on September 15, 2001. It was the first day after 9/11 that planes were again in the air. The country was in shock and mourning. Nepal is close to Pakistan, Afghanistan and India. After debating internally about whether I should leave, I called my mother and asked "Do you think I should go?"

"I've never been a worrier," said Mom. "Go and do what you need to do."

People of all faiths make pilgrimages. Mine was to the mountains of Nepal, others may journey to Lourdes or Mecca or a spiritual retreat center. Pilgrimages can be taken to a forest, or the ocean, or to a tree in your own backyard. You can design your own pilgrimage to discovery. Destination does not matter as much as your attitude. Are you seeking? Are you learning? Are you open to what you will find?

In Nepal I learned about "Phowa," the dying meditations. Meant to be used at the moment of death, Phowa is practiced throughout your life so that at the time of death you are ready to transcend. I have learned that before we can wake up to Life, we must first learn to die in many ways—to die to our old lives, our obsessive attachment to possessions, and to the way we want things to be. In learning to die, you begin to learn how to live.

I learned much from the monks in Nepal and Thailand that I would like to share with you. I cannot claim that I returned as an enlightened teacher, or that I now live fearlessly alive in the moment all the time. There are times I am still afraid and cling to safety nets. The questions of Will they like me? and Am I enough? still lurk and spring forth unbidden when I least expect it. Some mornings I hear the wake-up alarm, only to hit the snooze button and bury myself in the warm blankets once again. Like you, I still live in Saba.

Waking up to Life is not a one-step, one-size-fits-all process. It is a life-long adventure in which we must challenge ourselves daily and in every moment to live and love bigger. To seek that which is real, which is true. To seize and relish every precious moment.

Waking up may be easy or it may be difficult. It may happen in one glorious instant of enlightenment, or it may unfold over a lifetime. Waking up to Life is like devouring a fully ripe mango. It's juicy, fresh, luscious, and sometimes a little messy.

Know this—your life will change utterly when you wake up to your true Self. The Sufi poet Hafiz described his student's awakening in this way:

I once had a student
Who would sit alone in his house at night
Shivering with worries and fears.
Come morning,
He would often look as though
He had been raped by a ghost.

Then one day my pity
Crafted for him a knife
From my own divine sword.
Since then I have become very proud of this student.
For now, come night,
Not only has he lost all his fear,
Now he goes out
Just looking for Trouble.

Chapter 1

Taming the Monkey
Living with Awareness

Journal Entry 10/3/01

I'm staying in a guesthouse at a monastery high on a hill above Katmandu. Every morning at 5am I am roused by the sound of bells calling the monks—and me—to meditation. I am a guest here, so morning meditation is optional for me, and some mornings I groan, pull the covers over my head, and go back to sleep. And then I feel guilty. It took me days to figure out that the monks didn't care if I got up for morning meditation or not; they are just glad to have me here.

Everything is so different in Nepal, which is wonderful and distracting. There are monkeys in the villages, and I've been warned that they will aggressively steal food if they see you eating, so I try to be sneaky if I'm snacking while strolling through town—I take stealthy little bites and abruptly stop chewing if I hear monkey chatter nearby. Pushy monkeys are not something I've ever had to worry about before. I even heard a horror story about a woman being attacked by a large male who tried to ... um ... mate with her. What perfume was she wearing? I don't want any.

There are also lots of dogs, ducks, chickens, and goats running around the streets, and, of course, the sacred cows. Because cows are sacred here, they wander wherever they like at whatever speed they like. A cow standing in the middle of the street, placidly eating and staring blankly at honking cars and hooting people often holds up traffic. Although the right of way of cows is generally respected, occasionally a child will run out and switch its haunches with a stick to get it to move—just another example of human impatience with the sometimes maddeningly slow pace of the Divine will.

The monks are very kind and generous to me. They are always giving me little gifts: a cookie, a little coin purse, or a book to translate Tibetan. They are also very joyous, which is amazing since most of them escaped from Tibet and are now living in exile. They have lost everything and are rebuilding, and yet, their smiles light up a room.

The first step to waking up is to simply become more aware. Awareness is easy in certain situations: when we walk through a deep forest enjoying the scent of the trees, or when we pause to appreciate a sunset of remarkable beauty, or when taking in unfamiliar sights and sounds, as I did in Nepal.

But is it possible to be aware on a busy freeway driving to work? Can beauty be found in the line of cars, the smell of exhaust, and the expressionless faces of other drivers? What is gained by being aware of such familiar, and not entirely pleasant, scenes?

Here is a simple experiment that illustrates the benefits of awareness. Go into a familiar room in your house, the living room, or a bedroom, and cover the windows and turn out the lights so that the room is completely black. This is easiest to achieve at night. If you can't black out a room, blindfold yourself so that you cannot see your surroundings. Now try to locate a chair or object across the room.

Be warned that most people trying this exercise will bang into furniture, stub their toes, and knock over knickknacks. Where did that chair come from? Is that my dresser or the bedside table? Each bump and bruise provides more information about the room, so you can correct your course and eventually find what you are looking for.

Searching in the dark is a metaphor for life without awareness. There is a tendency to react to life, eyes closed to what surrounds you. You may eventually get where you want to go, but only as the result of great personal struggle—in other words, lots of bumps and bruises.

Now imagine that room by the light of a single candle. With even a tiny bit of light, you can navigate through the room, plan your way, avoid obstacles, and see the goal ahead. The more light you have, the easier it becomes. So it goes with awareness.

Have you ever misplaced your keys and thought you were losing your memory? You didn't actually "lose" your keys: you were not aware when you put them down. Had you felt the cold metal in your hand and watched with conscious awareness where you placed the keys, you would know exactly where to find them. Which leads me to ask:

What things, people, joys, and ideas in your life are you misplacing or forgetting?

How often do your thoughts wander away from what you are doing or whom you are with? It is easy to drive the familiar commute to work lost in daydreams. You may be thinking up clever comebacks for the argument you had with your spouse last night, or thinking about how to explain to the boss why you are late getting in, or planning what to make for dinner that night. Have you ever reached a destination and been completely unaware of anything you saw during the trip? Talk about the dangers of drunk driving—and unconscious driving!

The Buddha called the mind "a monkey," and "a wild horse." The monkey mind sets up a constant internal chatter— calculating and scheming, quarreling and debating, remembering wrongs against "me and mine." The wild horse mind loves to run away into fantasies and daydreams, to wander far without warning, and to return when it pleases.

Training the monkey and wild horse is a life-long project, but there are simple ways in which you can begin to still the chatter and increase your awareness every single day. Exercises designed to help you increase your awareness are scattered throughout this book. When you come to one, I encourage you to stop reading and write down the answers to the question posed or try the experiment suggested.

Another word for awareness is ***attention.*** By turning your complete attention to a problem, person, thing, or idea you immediately begin to increase your awareness. "The moment one gives close attention to anything, even a blade of grass, it becomes a mysterious, awesome, indescribably magnificent world in itself," writes Henry Miller. And, it is true.

Awareness of self

Habits are mindless acts that stunt growth and block awareness. And they are seductive. Habits often reduce pain or discomfort, which explains many addictions. Habits and addictions are ways we escape the discomforts of life. Observe yourself. What are you avoiding whenever you engage in a compulsive action? Whether a small habit like checking your cell phone, or a more destructive addiction like using drugs, notice which discomfort you are medicating in the present moment.

Some examples of habits: Drinking coffee in the morning, frequently checking email, getting up or going to bed at a certain time, eating meals at specific times. walking the dog, making to-do lists, folding towels a certain way, listening to music while exercising, voting for a particular party, having wine with dinner.

Note that any of these behaviors could also be consciously chosen (rather than done habitually). For example, if I consciously choose to drink coffee each morning, then that isn't a habit, it is a choice. However, beware, for it is very easy to fall into a routine and always make the safest, most familiar choice and thus, form a habit. Once you are aware of your habits, it is a good practice to purposely break them—choose to allow your body to rest and do without exercise for one day; go hiking instead of playing golf on Saturday; give up cigarettes, gum, alcohol or even food for a day. Do things differently and pay attention to how you feel.

What are your habits?

In a notebook or on a piece of paper, write down your habits. Include "good," "bad" and neutral habits, anything from exercising every day to biting your nails or smoking. Don't worry about why you do certain things and don't try to justify them—just write them down. Observe your behavior throughout the day and try to catch yourself indulging in any kind of pre-programmed behavior, then return to your notebook and add the habit to the list. Once you have a list of your habits, take a moment to reflect on them. Which of these habits are serving you, and which are causing you pain and suffering? Ask yourself, "Does this habit help me live my life the way I want to?" If not, it is time to make a different choice.

We also form *belief systems* based on subtle and obvious messages we have received from others, particularly our parents. We learn what to do in order to be successful and to be loved. We learn what is appropriate and inappropriate behavior, what is right and wrong.

Every sentence spoken, every action performed, is seeded by a belief and belief system. Listen for the messages reflected by your speech. Do your words echo paradigms of *I'm not good enough, I don't deserve better, the world is not a safe place,* or *I don't trust God?* What are the belief systems that are ruling your life?

It is important to recognize things you do and think which result from your belief systems. Bringing the belief systems that have formed you to the full light of awareness is not easy. The ego is sneaky and will try to present you with a justification for your behavior. As Nietzsche wrote: *"I have done that,* says my memory. *I cannot have done that* says my pride, and remains adamant."

In Nepal, I saw a group of young monks playing in the grass outside the monastery. From six-year-olds to teens, they laughed and whooped as they leapt into a big pile of grass, then tumbled out. Suddenly, I realized *they were doing gymnastics.* I spent much of my life in a gym and coaching gymnasts, and here, on this mountaintop, where I felt so far removed from that life, I was astounded to see these young students in their flame-red and gold robes doing gymnastics. As I moved closer, they waved and called out "Tashi delek!" their customary greeting.

Soon I was laughing with them, and then I did a cartwheel and motioned for them to do the same. At first, they were astonished and confused at their female American friend. Then, one by one, they followed suit, each doing a cartwheel, or as close to a cartwheel as they could come. Next I tried a handstand, then a somersault, and they mimicked my motions in a "follow-me" game of gymnastic stunts.

After several hours of flipping, spotting, and teaching, I was told through a translator that the monks wanted to begin gymnastics classes the next day, and I happily agreed. Once or twice a week for the next three weeks, I led the young monks through a series of exercises that delighted us all.

One day, my teacher, Rinpoche Tsognyi, came outside to instruct the monks in the art of debating. As I watched their debates, I secretly wished they would show him their new gymnastics skills. I knew he would be as amused and delighted with their new abilities, *and* I wanted him to see what *I* had taught the monks. I wanted him to recognize me as "special" and admire and appreciate my achievement.

I don't fault myself for my wish to be appreciated. It all stemmed from a belief system that I am not special enough without external praise and validation.

The point of self-awareness is not to condemn yourself for all of your little personality flaws, but rather to be aware of how your behavior patterns and habits shape the way you live. Awareness is observation without judgment. You don't have to beat your ego over the head. Just observe its antics and have a good laugh.

What are your beliefs?

In your notebook, write down as many things as you can remember about what your parents and teachers taught you as you were growing up. What were their belief systems about God, other people, nature, the world, achievement, work, love, communication? A belief system is any idea or thought, positive or negative, which was expressed to you as a truth. *Hard work is always rewarded. You must believe in Jesus in order to go to heaven. Men are never faithful and will leave you. You must treat your fellow man as yourself. Other races are not as good as ours. Plants and animals are here for human use. You must go to college to be successful. I am not OK*

Which of these beliefs do you still hold as true? Which ones can you consciously embrace, knowing that they are helping you be the person you want to be, and which ones are you ready to let go?

For the next week, write down any negative self-statement you hear yourself make, whether out loud or in your own mind. Recognize each one comes from a faulty belief system that you are carrying about yourself. Even if those beliefs originated in childhood, it is you that is now continuing to build and reinforce them. Most of these beliefs are self-judgments you are carrying around. Every time you judge yourself, you provide ammunition for your negative belief system. Self-judgment provides a tremendous amount of fuel for faulty belief systems.

After writing down your negative self-statements, look for patterns that reflect core beliefs, such as *I'm not OK, I don't trust life* or *things don't work out my way*. Find the most common four or five negative beliefs that are creating and controlling your life.

Note them all in your journal, and then re-write your new truth about each belief. Write it as a statement with both ownership and power. As you write your new truth, forgive yourself for continuing to judge yourself as less then you really are. Self-forgiveness is key here and will be talked about throughout this book. You must have compassion for yourself in order to heal from your childhood messages.

Here is a form you can use:

I forgive myself for judging me as not OK. I know I am the one creating that belief. My new truth is that I am perfect, enough, beautiful, and deserve the best of everything. I have nothing to worry about.

Or *I forgive myself for judging myself as fat. I know I am the one creating that belief. My new truth is that my body is beautiful, sexy, strong, and healthy. I am beautiful.*

Create a document or manifesto of your new truths. See them, read them, and say them often. Remember these beliefs create your reality. Create them mindfully.

In identifying your beliefs, it is not to blame your parents, family, teachers, and friends for helping to create those ways of thinking and acting. Resentment wastes time. In reality, many beliefs may be due to misinterpreted or inadequately understood messages. As a child, I saw my brothers get lots of attention and praise heaped on them for their accomplishments. That's when I decided that I needed to achieve in order to be loved. In reality, my parents loved all their children, and they were simply encouraging us to be the best we could be.

Freeing yourself of your "inner robot" is the first step in becoming a truly free and awake human being and a life filled with possibilities, choices, imagination and magic. It is the first step in not allowing faulty belief systems to control your life but SELF-determining who you are and what you want to create.

Awareness of others

The tribes of northern Natal in South Africa have a unique greeting, writes Peter Senge in his *Fifth Discipline Fieldbook*. Rather than just saying "hello," they call out, "Sawu bona" which means, "I see you." The traditional response is "Sikhona," which means, "I am here." The greeting formally acknowledges and respects the other person's existence. In the Zulu tribe, a common folk saying is "A person is a person because of other people."

The feeling that others do not see us is widespread in our culture. This is one of the most common sources of sadness I hear from patients as a therapist. We want more than to be needed, we want to be *seen*. We want to be recognized and respected for the unique individuals that we are.

In a workshop, I once became distraught over some personal issue and dissolved in tears before the group. I don't even remember now what was bothering me, but I do remember how the teacher brought me to awareness. He said "Alison, go to that mirror hanging on the wall and tell me what you see."

Standing before the mirror, I told him what I saw. "I see tears in my eyes, I see wrinkles, and my face is a little red and blotchy."

"Take another look," he suggested. "Then tell me what you see."

I began to search for the "right" answer to give him. Maybe he wanted me to look past my physical flaws at that moment. I said "I see the goodness in my eyes. I have a good heart."

A little impatiently, he said, "Look again and tell me what you see."

What did he want me to see? "I see myself as a searcher. I am trying to find something, to search for truth. I am trying to see past my present concerns."

"Alison," he demanded, "When are you going to notice the other twenty-nine people in the room?"

Shocked into silence, I shifted my gaze slightly and became aware of the reflected faces of all the others in the group staring at me in the mirror.

I turned to my teacher and gave the only appropriate response in that moment: "Thank you." How many times in my life have I been so caught up in myself that I didn't notice the eyes of another looking right at me, like those twenty-nine pairs of eyes in the mirror?

As I returned to my seat I felt guilty and humiliated. Why hadn't I seen it? As the workshop continued with another participant sharing, I remained stuck in my heady drama. Was the group mad at me? Did they think I was selfish? Suddenly a thought erupted like a bang: I WAS STILL DOING IT!

As the rest of the group turned their attention to another participant, I continued to ramble on about myself in my head. In beating myself up, I was keeping myself from being present and loving. With a quick laugh at myself, I turned my attention to the group member who was doing the sharing.

Often we are so caught up in our own life dramas, we have no time to notice what is going on with others. An aware life requires more than just awareness of self. We live with more than six billion other people on this tiny planet. Living with awareness means approaching others from a place of honor and respect. It means saying to them, like the tribes in Africa, "I see you." There is no other person or being that is as important as the one you are with now. Give that person your full attention. *See* them. Listen to the story they have to tell.

In connecting with other people, an energy exchange takes place. You affect them, and they affect you. With full attention, dynamic energy is exchanged in a loop, growing synergistically so that you both gain more energy than you contribute. If either or both of you become distracted, it is like yanking an electrical cord out of its socket—all energy flow immediately ceases.

Are you an energy giver or an energy taker?

The next time you enter a room, whether at home or work, pause a moment and think about the people on the other side of the door. Are you about to enter the room with grace and love, warmth and respect towards those present, or with criticism and judgment?

"We are one, after all, you and I," wrote the French scientist and priest Pierre Teilhard De Chardin. "Together we suffer, together exist, and forever will recreate each other."

Like a ripple from a stone thrown into a pond, we leave an energetic "fingerprint" or imprint on all we come into contact with. Others experience our imprints in every moment of our existence. We are continually either giving or taking energy from the world.

As a child one of my favorite toys was Silly Putty, which I pressed onto the Sunday newspaper comics to see the distorted image reflected in the clay as I peeled it off. Seeing that image again in my mind reminds me of the way I impact people every day. We are all mounds of Silly Putty. Some fresh and pink, others black by the imprints we have picked up from others. What imprints are you leaving on the world?

In Jerold Jampolsky's book, *Love is Letting Go of Fear,* he states very simply that when we interact in the world we either come from a place of love or a place of fear. All actions and choices, he writes, are simply outgrowths of these two basic emotions.

To increase my awareness of both self and others, I began a simple practice that I learned from a friend and recommend for you. Each morning I put twenty paper clips in my left pocket. As I interacted with others throughout the day, I would slow down and ask myself, "Is this coming from a place of love, or coming from a place of fear?" If I felt defensive, fearful, angry, or self-protective, I knew it was a fear response. Every time I acted out of fear, I took one of the paper clips out of my left pocket and put it in my right. Soon I found I could go several days without removing a paper clip from my left pocket.

After one month, I switched the paper clips from my left to my right pocket. Every time I responded from a place of love, consideration, caring, patience, or compassion, I switched the paper clips to my left side and began a "love clip" collection. As the month progressed and I got better at acting from a place of love, I ran out of paperclips by midday and needed to add more to my starter pocket.

Our energetic imprint on others happens even when they are unaware of us. If you snicker or roll your eyes at the sight of someone who is obese or loudly dressed—in other words, someone "different" than you—you might as well have walked up and slapped them in the face. We are always aware, even if unconsciously, of negative feelings aimed at us. We are beings of energy right down to the atoms that compose our bodies, and we are all affected by the energy that we encounter. Can't you feel it when someone in a bad mood walks into a room? Aren't you always at least subtly aware of someone else's disapproval of you?

We are one interconnected web. The Lakota Indian phrase "Mitakue oyasin," means *we are all related.* We all struggle to find happiness despite the suffering in this life. You have a common bond with the saint and the sinner, the philanthropist and the thief, the physician and the murderer.

"I'm not into isms and asms," said Dick Gregory. "There isn't a Catholic moon and a Baptist sun. I know the universal God is universal …. I feel that the same God-force that is the mother and father of the pope is also the mother and father of the loneliest wino on the planet."

As a human being, you belong to the wildest, most outrageous, loving, crazy, dysfunctional family on Earth! Everyone is your brother, sister, mother, father. Awareness of others means taking the words of the Bible seriously when Jesus says, "Love thy neighbor as thyself." That neighbor could be from another state, another sexual preference, another form of life, another religion. We must love as if we are all made of the same stuff—because we are. We are far more alike than we are different.

As long as there is a Me, there is separation. Awareness of others is realizing we are all interconnected and have an impact on the rest of humanity with our every thought and action.

Global Awareness

An astounding discovery by Dr. Masaru Emoto demonstrates how truly interconnected all of life is on this planet. His book *The Hidden Messages in Water* is an eye-opening theory showing how water is deeply connected to our individual and collective consciousness. Using high-speed photography, he discovered that crystals formed in frozen water differed according to where the water was found. Water from clear springs and sacred sites show brilliant, complex, and colorful snowflake patterns, while polluted water forms incomplete, asymmetrical patterns with dull colors

He then expanded the experiment by trying to influence the crystals with different types of music, visual images, and words written on paper. The water crystals responded and re-formed themselves according to different types of stimulus. Heavy metal music produced profoundly different crystals than

Tibetan folk songs or music by Enya. Words and phrases such as "I love you" or "Thank you," written in various languages, produced graceful, kaleidoscopic patterns rather than the muddy, incomplete crystals that formed to the words "I hate you" or "You make me sick."

In his final experiment, Emoto asked monks to pray and chant over muddy, polluted water. The water gradually "healed," until it once again formed into bright, clear crystals.

Emoto's experiments reveal the ability of water to absorb, hold, and even re-transmit human feelings and emotions. He theorizes that since water has the ability to receive a wide range of frequencies, it can also reflect the universe in this manner. Since people are seventy percent water, and the Earth is seventy percent water, Emoto believes we can heal our planet and ourselves by consciously expressing love and goodwill.

These experiments are dramatic examples of how intention, sound, and prayer can actually change physical matter. If water "reacts" to a song, word, or prayer, so must the food we eat, the plants in our homes and out in nature, the ocean, the earth, and humanity itself. The molecules of the food you eat and the water you drink actually changes when you consume them with gratitude.

Quantum theory says that atoms and even sub-atomic particles are involved in a constant exchange of energy. The web of life is conscious and alive—it grows, reacts and changes continually. "The properties of subatomic particles can therefore only be understood in a dynamic context; in terms of movement, interaction and transformation," writes Fritjof Capra.

The poets as well as the scientists recognize the

interconnectedness of all life. The poet from India, Rabindranath Tagore, described it in this way:

The same stream of life that runs through my veins night and day runs through the world and dances in rhythmic measures.

It is the same life that shoots in joy through the dust of the earth in numberless blades of grass and breaks into tumultuous waves of leaves and flowers.

It is the same life that is rocked in the ocean-cradle of birth and death, in ebb and in flow.

I feel my limbs are made glorious by the touch of this world of life. And my pride is from the life-throb of ages dancing in my blood this moment.

You are part of a jigsaw puzzle here on earth. Each piece of the puzzle is separate, each piece is unique, and each piece interacts with and contributes to the whole.

How do you live as part of the Global Community?

"You must understand the whole of life, not just one little part of it," writes Krishnamurti. "That is why you must read, that is why you must look at the skies, that is why you must sing, and dance, and write poems, and suffer, and understand, for all that is life."

To know your part in the puzzle, you must be aware of what's going on in the world. Don't accumulate just the facts that support your own worldview. Challenge yourself. This week, read a newspaper or magazine with a different perspective from your own. If you are liberal, find a conservative paper or vice versa. I have found that even just listening to the BBC's (British Broadcasting Corporation) version of world news is eye-opening. Their take on world events is often very different than that of the U.S. media—even though Britain is one of our closest allies!

Challenge yourself to learn. Read about science, history, politics, ecology, religion, spirituality. Read children's stories and read novels that are set in unfamiliar circumstances or locales. Read poetry.

Become consciously aware of the food you eat, the water you drink, the grass you step on, and the bugs you kill. Say small prayers of gratitude for all the creatures on the planet. Say a blessing out loud or to yourself before eating anything. It's a good way to wake up and break out of unconscious eating!

Thich Nhat Hanh suggests a "tangerine meditation" to become more aware of what you are eating. You can do this meditation with any type of food, and I have used raisins with workshop participants.

One day, I offered a number of children a basket filled with tangerines. The basket was passed around, and each child took one tangerine and put it in his or her palm. We each looked at our tangerine, and the children were invited to meditate on its origins. They saw not only the tangerine, but also its mother, the tangerine tree. With some guidance, they began to visualize the blossoms in the sunshine and in the rain. Then they saw petals falling down and tiny green fruit appear. The sunshine and the rain continued, and the tiny tangerine grew. Now someone has picked it, and the tangerine is here. After seeing this, each child was invited to peel the tangerine slowly, noticing the mist and the fragrance of the tangerine, and then bring it up to his or her mouth and have a mindful bite, in full awareness of the texture and taste of the fruit and the juice coming out. We ate slowly like that.

Each time you look at a tangerine, you can see deeply into it. You can see everything in the universe in one tangerine. When you peel it and smell it, it's wonderful. You can take your time eating a tangerine and be very happy.

Human actions and lack of awareness lead to destruction on a grand scale—acid rain has destroyed millions of acres of rainforest; rivers and seas have literally died from pollution; the ozone layer is no longer able to protect us from the sun's harmful rays as it has done in the past; and extravagant energy use has created global warming and climactic changes.

If you become more informed about the world you live in, you can make conscious choices about where you contribute your energy and your money. Where do you spend your money? What companies do you support? Who is exploiting the world's people and resources? We must be willing to look beyond the immediate comfort of ourselves as individuals and act in ways that protect and enhance the future for ourselves *and* every other being on this astounding planet.

Spiritual Awareness

"You are not a human being in search of spiritual experience. You are a spiritual being immersed in a human experience," said Pierre Teilhard de Chardin.

A final form of awareness is subtler than all the rest—the awareness of the Realized Self.

The Realized Self is you in your most divine spiritual essence. Some may call it your higher self or your soul. The Realized Self watches this world from a point of detachment high above the action. The Realized Self is the observer of your persona. If you are aware of your Realized Self, you have the ability to get out of the drama and into the truth.

Spiritual Awareness is the knowledge that everything is moving on the perfect path for your evolution—an amazing trust in the web of life and the part you play in it. Spiritual awareness is the ultimate in trust and letting go. It is the part of you that understands all adversity is opportunity, and all events are open to interpretation. Everything changes. If you step into a river today, it will not be the same river you crossed last year, or even ten seconds ago. The web of life is in constant flux, expanding and contracting, ebbing and flowing, as Life is constantly created and re-created.

You are woven into this web. You are not alone. Trust Life. Trust God, or your Higher Self, or the Universe to nourish you with what you need to grow. Guidance comes in little ways when we are listening with spiritual awareness.

How wonderful it would be if we all could live from this perspective! If we all understood that there are no "bad" things and that everything is a vehicle to practicing a higher form of love, wisdom, and compassion. When you are spiritually aware, you are truly free because you have no fear of outcome. You know everything is perfect. There is no need to doubt, or struggle. Everything is as it should be.

When have you received Guidance?

It is not always easy to see difficult circumstances as leading to your greater good, but it is possible when viewed from the perspective of the Realized Self. In your notebook, write down three painful or difficult events that later worked out to your greater good—times when something good came from something bad, or times when you received help and caring just when you thought all was lost.

Spiritual awareness is seeing the divinity of all things. All things, not only the good things. From lost jobs, to lost loves, all events in life are manifestations of the Divine. With spiritual awareness, you understand that God or the Universe or the Greater Self is working on your behalf even if you don't understand it at this moment. Trust in life. Martin Luther King Jr. said "I believe in the sun even when it isn't shining. I believe in God even when He is silent."

All things are blessed.

Everything. Every event, every person, every creature, every rock, tree and star grants you the opportunity to increase your awareness, to awaken to the magic that is your life. When you can see your life from a spiritual perspective, you have a bird's eye view that allows wisdom and insight to manifest.

With the heightened view of the Realized self, you can watch your own drama unfold as if on a stage or movie screen. You experience triumph and tragedy, wins and losses, as the plot develops. Other characters interact with yours, bringing their own dramatic and funny moments to the arc of the story. The Buddha suggested that suffering is lessened—or at least understood with awareness—if you can view the events of your life with this sense of detachment.

One day in 1999, I lay on my couch feeling as if I would die—as if my heart would explode inside my chest. I had experienced an unendurable loss, a loss that I did not think I could survive.

I met the first true love of my life at age 33. This was a big love. For a year we had attempted to love each other in a way we called "Butterfly in the Hand." A butterfly can be held gently in an open palm, but if you try to prevent its flight by closing your fingers around it, you will crush it. We vowed that we would love without fear, jealousy, or holding back. We loved with all our hearts even at the risk that some day it might end. We loved as if each day was to be our last day together. I was ready for such a love, or so I thought. I had done years of therapy and spiritual practice, I had had other good relationships, I was solid in my self.

Yet the person I believed to be my life partner became restless and took wing. Now I lay on a couch in my apartment curled in a fetal position. Wounded animal cries emerged from my throat.

As I lay there wailing, a strange thing happened. I felt myself float out of my body as I had done so many times in my meditation practice. From this vantage point, I began to simply observe myself and my pain. I watched the heroine of the movie devastated after losing the love of her life. Soon I found myself saying to her, "You go, girl! Experience this pain. This is what you came down here for. To live big and to love big. What did you want, anyway, some mediocre life, with half-baked emotions? A so-so movie? Cry! And know that this is all part of the big beautiful process."

When we look at the world and our lives from a place of spiritual awareness we are able to trust our lives and act from our highest selves. We recognize the divinity of all events and trust that each event is a learning experience designed to let us live bigger and freer. We realize that any event that causes us discomfort or a negative feeling in our body is a messenger showing us a part of us that needs healing. We see the wounds we have from our faulty belief systems, and have the awareness to go inside to heal ourselves from our pain and discomfort.

As awareness increases, we cease arguing with our lives, cease clinging to the notion that we have somehow been wronged. Struggle eases and flow increases. Practice living your life from the higher viewpoint of the Observer.

Life is so much easier with the grace and wisdom of spiritual awareness. It's what you came down here to experience. You are a spiritual being having a human experience.

Chapter 2

Grab Your Paintbrush
Living with Intention

Journal Entry 10/24/01

As I walked down the hill to town this afternoon, there was an old monk walking up the path toward me. He was bent far over, picking at the dirt path with a stick. He seemed to be looking for something. Occasionally he would stop and gently fling dirt over to the side of the road. I wondered "What is he doing, bent over like that, walking so slow?" As I approached him, I saw that he was finding earthworms that had been flooded out by last night's hard rain. He was gently picking them up and saving them from being trampled by moving them to safety in the grass next to the path. He looked up as I approached, said, "Namaste" with a big smile, and continued his task.

Every moment you make a choice. Every moment is filled with intentions. And every moment these choices and intentions create your life—and contribute to the sum of life on earth—the lives of the people, the lives of creatures, the life of the planet.

Thich Nhat Hanh, a Buddhist monk, says that everything we do can be an act of poetry or art if we do it with mindfulness and intention. "Even when we are not painting or writing, we are still creating. We are pregnant with beauty, joy, and peace, and we are making life more beautiful for many people." He describes how even the simple act of walking can impact the earth. When you walk fast with anger or worry-filled thoughts, you are imprinting anxiety and sorrow on the earth. However, if you form the intention "to kiss the earth with your feet," you imprint serenity and peace.

Today is a fresh new day. It is the first day you have, the last day you have, and the only day you have. In this moment, you have the opportunity to create whatever you want. Your intention is your act of creation. Imagine your life as a blank slate: an artist's canvas waiting for its first illuminating splash of paint. Today you can create your masterpiece. Your mind is your paintbrush, and you are in charge of it. What do you want to create today?

If your days drift by without setting definite intention, your life becomes directionless, without much structure or purpose. The paintbrush moves, smearing random colors which, sometimes, with luck, produce a splendid image, but which more often mix by chance to become shapeless muddy gray impressions.

The importance of mental discipline and intention can be demonstrated by a classic exercise which I use in my work with companies and athletes. Each participant is given a string with a fishing weight tied to the end. Sitting at a table with their elbows cocked at a ninety-degree angle to the tabletop, one hand firmly grasping the other wrist to prevent any conscious movement, they dangle the string and weight. Then I tell them to visualize the weight swinging from side to side and say the words "side to side" in their mind over and over again. To their amazement, the weight begins to swing from side to side. If they then change their conscious intention to "forward and back," the weight "miraculously" follows suit. The swing of the weight changes direction with a simple change of intention. That is the power of the mind: to create an event as the result of conscious intention.

Our thoughts literally create our lives. Our words and actions, our choices and intentions spring both consciously and unconsciously from our belief systems, as we saw in Chapter One. Buddha recognized this truth more than 2,500 years ago when he said:

> *The thought manifests as the word; The word manifests as the deed; The deed develops into habit; And habit hardens into character. So watch the thought and its ways with care, And let it spring from love born out of concern for all beings.....We are shaped by our thoughts; we become what we think.*

In Buddhism, Right Thought, Right Speech and Right Action are three of the steps on the Noble Eightfold Path. You direct your life through thought, word, and action. Forming your intention as to how you will think, speak, and act in each moment and throughout your day is both creative and powerful.

Intention requires focus. Have you ever tried to ignite paper or a piece of wood using a magnifying glass? If you keep moving the glass, even the magnified power of the sun's beams through the lens will not start a fire. But if you hold the magnifying lens perfectly still, you can harness the power of the sun by focusing the rays in a concentrated beam of energy— and you will ignite a fire.

Decide and develop a *laser-like focus* on who you want to be, what energies and results you want in your life, and the necessary actions to make it happen. Your intention begins to create everything you imagine. Be disciplined. Don't allow yourself to stay stuck in negative thoughts.

Are you ready to set intention?

Are you ready to create a new world designed by your intentions? The first step is to aim a specific, laser-like focus on what you intend to create. Sit quietly alone for a moment. A quiet period in the morning is good, perhaps when you first awake. Take out your notebook and answer these three questions to determine your intention for the day ahead.

Who do I want to be today?

Do you want to be loving and energetic? Or relaxed and confident? What words describe the person you want to create today? Even if your day is filled with must-do chores and stress, you can decide to approach them in such a way as to fill your life with grace or misery. Who do you want to be today as a wife, husband, sister, brother, child, co-worker? Who do you want to be as you walk into work? As you walk in the door to your home?

What do I want to accomplish?

The answer to this question can range from "nothing" to any number of tasks on your daily list. Setting intention about concrete tasks focuses your attention and allows you to recognize ways you are moving forward. Setting intention is also establishing your spiritual tasks for the day. What do you want to accomplish in order to move your soul forward? Being more patient, expressing your love to someone dear, listening patiently rather than interrupting, treating a stranger you meet or a clerk in the store as a Very Important Person?

Does this behavior represent my highest self?

Life is like a continuous pop quiz. Will you show up for the test? Are you being who you were born to be? In every situation you have an opportunity to manifest yourself exactly as you want to be. Remember: *love or fear.* Your highest self is one that matches your value system. Most likely, it exemplifies an attitude of love, trust, compassion, kindness, and truth. Ask yourself if your behavior represents your highest self in every interaction.

One of the greatest gifts the universe gives us is the opportunity for "do-overs." Every moment is fresh. Every moment is new. If you make a decision or act in a way that doesn't represent your highest self, you always have an opportunity to do it over in the next moment. If you find yourself angry and yelling at a co-worker, you can always stop, apologize, smile, and continue the discussion in a friendly manner. How wonderful it is that we can keep on wiping the slate clean and create the next moment with much clearer intention.

If the events and happenings of the day begin to overwhelm you, the first thing to do is *slow down*. Pause and take a few deep, slow breaths before you set an intention to create exactly what you want in both your words and actions. Rushing often leads to reactions that we later regret, whether it is harsh words to a child or saying "yes" to something we cannot possibly handle in our already jam-packed lives.

Lama Surya Das recommends an excellent way to remember and re-focus your intentions throughout the day. Create your own mottos and watchwords, or write down some you've heard that are significant to you. "Try to mine your own life for the wisdom sayings that resonate with your heart," writes Surya Das. "Your life and your path are unique; why not have a few unique slogans that have meaning to you?" Write down your slogans and carry them around with you, perhaps in your pocket or purse. Some of these might be your new truths from Chapter One.

Surya Das stuck a lapel pin to the dashboard of his car that says, *Celebrate Life*. "I like having it there to remind Serious Das to lighten up and find joy in whatever needs to be done."

Setting intention is your road map for life. Decide who you want to be as an executive, mother, father, manager, student, artist, and don't let anything take you off that mark. The intention you set for yourself not only keeps your own life on track, with no regrets, it also impacts others every day. When you set intention, your life becomes a creation instead of simply a reaction. Speak mindfully, act thoughtfully, and see your life change. You are the Creator.

Intentional speech

Words are some of the most powerful symbols we have. We are bombarded with words every day—from television, talk radio, advertisements, politicians, children, spouses, coworkers, and friends—careless words, loving words, angry words, thoughtful words, destructive, or inspirational words.

How do you want to use your words?

Your words can be weapons or gifts to the world. They can be mindless chatter or poetry. All the words that fall from your mouth create an imprint on the web on life. Form an intention to only use words that are true to your higher Self. Words that are clear, honest, sincere and uplifting rather than toxic to yourself and others. It can help to pause before speaking and ask yourself: Is this true? Is this necessary? Is it kind?

Sometimes it is best to say nothing. Communication would be improved if sometimes we just shut our mouths and engaged in what Thich Nhat Hanh calls compassionate listening.

"Compassionate listening brings about healing," he writes. "When someone listens to us this way, we feel some relief right away. We have to learn to do the same in order to heal the people we love and restore communication with them."

To listen compassionately is to listen deeply to another's words, to try to understand what meaning they are trying to express, without judgment or reservations, without mentally planning our advice or rebuttal while we are listening. It is not always easy to do, but compassionate listening will change your relationships in ways you can't imagine.

Your words are your thoughts spoken aloud. Without clear, focused intention before you speak, you might find your monkey mind is chattering away loudly before you have even consciously decided what to say.

Speak the Truth

How often do you lie? If we examine our words honestly, we will usually realize that we are perhaps not as honest as we think. We lie to avoid conflict. We lie to save our skin. We lie to make ourselves seem stronger or more important. How many times have you not told the "whole" truth in order to avoid confrontation or to save face?

Socially approved "little white lies" keep us trapped in a maze of illusion. We create a house of mirrors where, lie-by-lie, our lives become distorted and warped. At first the lies seem okay: "I didn't want to hurt her feelings," or "I couldn't deal with his reaction," or "I don't want her to think I'm an idiot!" But these lies disrupt the positive flow of cause and effect in our lives, and they poison and distort our integrity in the world. Deep inside, you know when you are lying, and others do as well.

For example, a man named John is cheating on his wife. He's been having affairs on and off for several years. John assures himself that it would be more painful for his wife to know the truth. He is afraid to endanger a marriage that is comfortable and financially stable. He eases his conscience by telling himself, "I still give her attention. It doesn't affect our relationship and she's happy with our comfortable life and our children." Living a lie is painful for all involved. John's wife can feel the lack of intimacy in their relationship. She knows something is missing and wonders what's wrong with her.

Don't fool yourself that withholding the truth serves you in any way. People know and can sense your lack of integrity.

Challenge yourself to find creative ways to be honest. Speaking honestly does not mean you should be harsh or cruel. "We can describe the truth in different ways to help different listeners understand our meaning," writes Thich Nhat Hanh, "but we must always be loyal to the truth."

When you feel you must express a truth that may be either misinterpreted or hurtful, pause to first form a clear intention. Are you speaking because you wish to clearly communicate with another, or are you coming from a place of fear or the need to prove you're "right?" The more you can shove your own ego out of your way, the easier truth-telling will become. Focus on the other person's eyes and concentrate on communicating from your higher Self to their higher Self, from a place of compassion and kindness. You may also find humor helpful as one way to take the sting out of harsh news. Use humor wisely, however, because it can also hurt feelings if the person feels you are being sarcastic or laughing at *them* rather than the *situation*.

Telling a big fish story

We all exaggerate. "Some people are so addicted to exaggeration that they can't tell the truth without lying," says humorist Josh Billings. Exaggeration can be as poisonous and damaging as outright lies, particularly when employed as gossip to make us feel superior to others. Exaggerations can also be little lies that make us feel better, or seem more important, or gain sympathy from others. Temporarily. But underneath every exaggeration is the belief system: "I don't feel good about myself, so I need to get that feeling from you." Others sense this message lurking under the exaggeration.

Think about the times you tend to exaggerate—whether it's complaining about the "hours and hours" of paperwork you had to do at the office or magnifying a minor accomplishment into a major achievement. Were others really impressed?

The comedian Ellen DeGeneres often satirizes our tendency to exaggerate during her monologues, saying things like, "I want to answer a question that everyone has been asking me … alright, only a few people have asked me … okay, nobody has asked me, but I want to tell you anyway …" DeGeneres shows that you can change course right in the middle of an exaggeration, come back to the truth, and people will respond to your ability to be truthful and laugh at yourself.

Are you a truth-teller?

Think back over your intentions and your actual behavior at the end of the day, particularly before you go to sleep. Write in your notebook any time at which you caught yourself telling a lie. Ask yourself, "Why did I lie?" and "What am I afraid of?" Note any instances of exaggeration during the day and describe your intention. Did you want to impress, gain sympathy, or protect yourself?

Not too much, not too little

Wise speech means choosing words with mindfulness and skill. Remember Emoto's experiments with the effect of words and prayers on water? Your words and the intention behind them *matters* to the rest of creation.

Are your words kind or cutting? Are they honest or sarcastic? Are you using humor to laugh at yourself or a situation, or is it at the expense of another? Are you saying too little or saying too much? Speaking with clarity and intention conveys a message that you are strong, confident, and clear. How many times have you talked with a person and found yourself drifting as they chatter on and on about something that could have been said in two sentences? How often have you seen someone else's eyes glaze over as you prattle on and on about something you could have conveyed in a few words?

A good practice is "laser language." Lasering your language means speaking clearly and succinctly, having consideration for your listener and how much they need to hear at the time. It is awareness of your listener's interest and timetable, so you can convey your message concisely. Lasering does not mean being uninteresting, or never telling a story. It's simply an awareness of the other person's attention and needs. Being skillful with speech is knowing when to laser, and knowing when to tell a story filled with color and detail. In the right situation, your long, drawn-out tale of adventure is exactly what everyone is waiting to hear!

Your words can make others feel like trash or like the most important person in the world. Encourage and uplift others by expressing the positive things you see about them and their lives. Use your words to make your world a more positive place. How can you change your day and the days of others, simply by being kind, enthusiastic, positive, and interested? This week, try spreading kindness and energy in your life and watch the changes. It's a great experiment!

Intentional Action

Your actions show what kind of life you are creating. "Right Action" as a Buddhist principle means acting to create harmony rather than conflict, and to spread love and compassion rather than fear and destruction. Every action is motivated by one of two emotions: love or fear. All our attitudes and feelings stem from these two basic emotions. Love inspires feelings from the heart and divine self, including joy, trust, compassion, sympathetic joy, excitement, interest, and encouragement. Fear generates feelings from the ego or childish self. These include hate, jealousy, anger, competition, possessiveness, and judgment. Our actions come from these feelings.

If your actions do not reflect your highest Self, you can actually create dis-ease in the body. In his book *Cancer as a Turning Point*, Lawrence Le Shan interviewed hundreds of people with terminal illnesses such as cancer. His startling conclusion was that the leading cause of terminal illness was despair. The people he spoke with were not living lives true to themselves. When those sufferers actively transformed their lives to become the people they wanted to be, to "sing their own song," as he put it, they often recovered from their disease.

Stop for a minute and think about what LeShan's study means in your own life. You may not have a terminal illness, but actions that leave you with negative feelings about yourself can still cause disease in the body. Behaviors resulting from fear and its many variables—anger, worry, jealousy, desperation, hate—can poison your body and result in insomnia, high blood pressure, stomach disorders, heart disease, destructive addictions, and ultimately, terminal illness.

When you experience negative emotions resulting from fear, the brain sends messages throughout the body to initiate the "fight or flight" response. Heart rate increases. Digestive functions are suppressed. Muscles tense up. Immune function is suppressed. All this is an effort to prepare the body to run or fight. The body does not know whether you are reacting to real physical danger or merely imagining fearful situations.

Try this experiment.

Close your eyes and vividly imagine a time when you felt totally in flow with life—a time when you felt that you were truly at home and at peace with yourself. It may have been a time of incredible joy or love. It may have been a time when you felt compassion or trust in another. Close your eyes and take a moment to reflect on that time. Feel again the joy of being in that place.

Now think about a time you acted out of fear, anger, or jealousy. Remember the event clearly. Feel all the feelings you felt at that time. It might be a time you said something or acted in a way you regretted. It might be a time you were jealous, insecure, or competitive. Remember those feelings in all their intensity now.

How did your body feel in both situations? What did it feel like when your actions were based in love and in harmony with your true Self, compared to when your actions came from a base attitude of fear? You only did this exercise for one minute. Think of the physical effect if you held those negative feelings for hours, days, or even years. Feelings of hate, anger, and jealousy actually poison our bodies. That is why right action is so important. Not just for what you can do in the world, but for what you do to your own life and body.

Right action is congruent with your values. When action matches values, everything is at ease. Everything is in the flow. Dis-ease comes when action is not congruent with the values you have set for yourself. Whenever your actions do not match your values, your body, as well as the entire web of life, suffers a little bit.

Unfinished Business

Incongruent or dishonest behavior often results in "leftovers." These leftover feelings are called unfinished business. Unfinished business is like garbage that hasn't been taken out for a while: it stinks, and the smell tends to fill everything. Unfinished business includes things you wish you had done, or said, such as apologies, expressing love, or taking a new job. Unfinished business between people tends to build up to an inevitable explosion.

Here's how it works. Let's say you have an argument with your husband or wife. You are angry, and try to talk it through, but it ends with both parties hurt and upset. You drop the argument, but still carry resentment about some of the things your partner said to you. How could s/he say that? Why is s/he so insensitive? Soon, everything your partner does reminds you of this thoughtlessness. A few days later your partner makes an innocent remark, and you react with a heated explosion of how selfish s/he is and how s/he doesn't care about your feelings. Unfinished business creates explosive reactions.

Think about times you have "stored up" points to prove you're right rather than just facing up to a situation. Unless you act on your feelings right away, you are in danger of overreacting to a minor irritation. Clean up as much unfinished business as possible. It may be small. A phone call left unreturned, a debt unpaid. Or it may be big. A long-term resentment. An apology left unsaid. Cleaning up unfinished business is like having a garage sale. It cleans out the clutter, creates new space, and gives you room to breathe. It is the cure for a heavy heart. You'll be amazed with how light your life feels when you deal with unfinished business.

Make a commitment today to clean up unfinished business.

Write in your notebook in the morning how you will begin to clean out some of the garbage, clutter or other "leftovers" in your life that are weighing you down.

Forming Intentions with Prostrations

After our first meeting at the Nepal monastery, my teacher gave me several "assignments" that would fill my days at the monastery, including meditations, readings, chanting, visualizations, and prostrations.

Prostrations are an ancient practice designed to purify our hearts and change our mindsets from a "me-centered" world of pride and ego to a more universal perspective of humility and respect. The Buddhist Lama Gendyn Rinpoche says we do prostrations with the intent to purify ourselves of pride and all past situations where we did not respect others. "Prostrations help us realize that there is something more meaningful than ourselves. In this way we purify the pride that we have accumulated through countless lifetimes thinking: *I am right, I am better than others*, or *I am the most important one*.

Prostrations are full body bows in which five points of the body touch the earth. We use them to form intentions on the level of body, speech, and mind.

In Nepal, I did prostrations five times a day in sets of one hundred at a time. There was a special prostration board on my balcony overlooking the Nepal countryside. In the morning, before sunrise, I would dress and put socks on both my feet *and* hands to help me slide out into a full body bow on my wooden board. I would do one hundred prostrations as the sun rose, another set of one hundred mid-morning, another one hundred near noon, another one hundred in the early afternoon, and, many days, my last one hundred prostrations were completed after sundown.

A simple way of doing prostrations is this: Begin by standing or kneeling with hands clasped in a prayer position. The traditional Buddhist approach is to then focus on the refuge tree, which is a detailed Tibetan image of a tree rising out of a beautiful lake. Represented in the image are teachers and buddhas from the past, present and future, as well as stacks of prayer books containing holy teachings. On the grassy shores of the lake are all our fellow beings (human and otherwise), who are our friends and enemies, family and strangers, all who exist with us on this earth presently and in the past and future. You mentally take refuge in this tree, and imagine that all these other beings are simultaneously taking refuge with you.

If you have never seen the image of a refuge tree, you can simply visualize a magnificent tree with great arching branches, and envision those who are taking refuge under it. I pictured a tree standing before me with sacred teachers, friends, and family in it, and I would dedicate each prostration to a different group or to individual people. Lama Gendyn Rinpoche believes that we must also "imagine the ones we consider our enemies in front of us, between the refuge tree and ourselves. We think of the people who cause us problems and obstruct the realization of our plans. All these people are very important because they help us develop such qualities as patience and compassion. We usually want to avoid such people. We try to stay away from them. We do not want to think about them. Putting them in front of us helps us not to forget them."

I visualized friends, family, enemies, people with AIDS, the homeless, anyone I could think of. Since this was just after 9/11, I visualized the souls of the dead, their families, Bin Laden, the suicide bombers and their families, and the workers helping the injured.

With the refuge tree image in your mind's eye, and your hands in prayer position, briefly touch your forehead, your throat, and then heart with an intention or prayer of purifying your body, speech, and mind. There is a symbolic meaning to these gestures. As you touch your forehead ask the people under the refuge tree for the blessing of their bodies, imagining rays of energy that radiate through your body and dissolve all its shadows and blocks. When your clasped hands touch your throat, ask for the blessing of enlightened speech. As you touch your heart, ask those gathered under the refuge tree for the blessing of the enlightened mind.

As you continue to visualize the tree, place the palms of your hand on the ground and slide into a full bow, stretching your body out as far as possible with your hands in a prayer position over your head. Your body should touch the ground with its five points (knees, hands, forehead), signifying that five negative emotions—anger, attachment, ignorance, pride, and jealousy—will leave your body and dissipate into the earth. Then slide back, and press the floor with your palms and get up. Return to your original position and begin another prostration.

This is a powerful practice that can be used daily in your life. Prostrations should be done mindfully and with focused intention. Start with a number that feels comfortable (or a little uncomfortable) for you and add from there.

With every prostration I felt my hardness crumble. With every bow I would say to those under the refuge tree, "I dedicate my life to the alleviation of your suffering." There were times I would cry as I bowed: from fatigue, from conviction. I cried as my aching body and aching heart pleaded for opening.

I remember seeing an old man doing Cora around the great Stupa. Cora is a walking circular meditation around the sacred site. Hundreds of people would gather for this meditation in the early morning and at sunset. This man must have been around seventy years old and did full body prostrations with every step around the stone circle. There were times I would think of him and dedicate my life and prostration practice to his inspiration.

If there was anything that helped me shed my hardened skin in Nepal, it was this amazing practice. I could feel my soul begin to blossom, and I felt humbled by the blessings I received. I have never felt so at peace and purposeful as when I performed this practice. With every dedication, I felt the energy of compassion traveling across the miles to those in need.

Intention as a State of Flow

"In the universe there is an immeasurable, indescribable force which shamans call intent, and absolutely everything that exists in the entire cosmos is attached to intent by a connecting link,." writes Carlos Casteneda

Intention is not only a decision or a mind-set. Intention is a force in the Universe that holds us and guides us along a Divine path. Imagine intention as a river surrounding us and carrying us downstream. We can choose which forks of the river to take or how long to stay in a slow or fast current, but no matter what choices we make, this river is carrying us to a Divine destination. We definitely feel it when we are paddling upstream, going against the strong current. Intention in this broader sense tells us that our lives are blessed and are moving toward a Divine conclusion even if we fight the current. No matter how much we flail about, no matter how many twists and turns our course takes, a Divine hand is guiding us and will not fail to work in our lives and bring us home. Intention is the power of creation; the divine will that maintains sustain us in our lives. Some people might call it God, others Love, but whatever you call this life force, know that it will ultimately ensure that goodness and virtue prevail in this universe.

In his beautiful book, *The Power of Intention*, Wayne Dyer talks about intention as the "trolley strap" of the universe. When we reach out and grab onto the flow of intention, we are connected with Source energy and our lives feel guided and blessed. We feel inspired and on course. When we are disconnected from this Source, we tend to feel afraid, stressed, and competitive. We are more likely to wonder why we are here and not trust where we are heading. Being unified with the power of intention does not mean our lives are predestined or there is no free will. It means that Divine intention has the ability to work good out of all situations, and we cannot thwart the Divine purpose with our free choices—not that some choices aren't better than others, for ourselves and for the good of the universe. We can purposely choose to assist Divine intention by living our lives with purpose and meaning.

Obstacles to connecting with Intention

What keeps us from connecting with the Divine Source? The ego. Our egos talk to us constantly and the monologue tends to be negative and untrue. It keeps us from connecting with the Divine. Our egos tend to lead us toward competition and separation from others rather than toward intentional love and connection. Wayne Dyer has identified six ego beliefs that keep us disconnected from the flow of Divine intention. When these six beliefs control our thinking, we find ourselves struggling and suffering:

1. *I am what I have.* My possessions define me.

2. *I am what I do.* My achievements define me.

3. *I am what others think of me.* My reputation defines me.

4. *I am separate from everyone.* My body defines me as alone.

5. *I am separate from all that is missing in my life.* My life space is disconnected from my desires.

6. *I am separate from God.* My life depends on God's assessment of my worthiness.

When I first arrived in Nepal, I was frustrated that everything happened so slowly. I had a fantasy in my head of how my adventure *should* be: I would arrive in Nepal, go to the guesthouse, and there I would find a teacher who would come up to me and say, "Alison, I've been waiting for you. I had a dream you would find me. Come with me to the mountain monastery and I will be your teacher."

After four days and no miraculous appearance by my teacher, I was very impatient. "Hello? I'm here! Where is my teacher? I've been waiting four days now!" Then, during a meditation session, I felt my controlling ego melt a little bit. I began to stop my struggling and trust the Divine source, and I realized my "teacher" was manifesting all around me. My days began to be filled with joy as I recognized new sources of wisdom, rather than with frustration because these sources weren't the ones I had planned for and desired. When I let go of my ego and opened my heart, I began to see the beauty of my surroundings, make new connections, and ultimately I found a teacher. The proverb I had heard many times proved to be true, when you truly let go, what you want suddenly appears!

How to Connect to Intention

"Everything you see has its roots in the unseen world," writes the poet Rumi. "The forms may change, yet the essence remains the same. Every wonderful sight will vanish, every sweet word will fade, but do not be disheartened, the source they come from is eternal, growing, branching out, giving new life and new joy. Why do you weep? The source is within you, and this whole world is springing up from it."

Getting in touch with the flow of connection is as easy and difficult as helping fish feel water. It is all around you. Notice the divinity in each moment. What is its beauty? What is its gift? Source energy is made up of the most powerful energies on earth. The energies of creation: Joy, Love, Openness, and Trust. Look for these in your life. Ask yourself. How can I love more in this moment? How can I live with more trust that there is a plan for creation? What can I learn from being open to what's happening in this moment? These nine attitudes will help you connect to the Divine flow of intention and break out of ego limitations:

... I trust Life and know there are Divine guidance and a plan for the universe.

... I know I only attract what I give energy to. I refuse to focus on negativity, anger, fear, or arguing. I know that focusing on these things further attracts them to me.

...   I know nothing in my life is entirely hopeless or evil. I use all adversity as opportunity and appreciate the gifts presented to me in every situation.

...   I know this is an abundant world with enough for everyone. When I am connected and on-purpose, abundance comes to me.

...   Creation is as it must be and should be. God makes everything perfect.

...   My well-being is not contingent upon ANY external circumstance.

...   I can learn something from every person I meet. I honor everyone as my teacher.

...   I trust my intuition and know my life is flowing perfectly.

...   I am interconnected to all that is. We are all part of the same energy and power.

Here's a practice I do that you can try. Each week, choose one of the nine beliefs listed above. Write it on several pieces of paper and put the saying in as many places as you can. Be sure you can see one from almost everyplace you are during the day: the car, computer screen, and bathroom mirror are all good places. Say the belief over and over again to yourself during the week. Consciously create that belief in your life.

Spend ten minutes in the morning and night focusing on your breathing and stating one of the nine beliefs as a meditation. You can also do this with your new written truths. Soon you will find yourself interpreting events and relationships differently, with more optimism and compassion.

When I first became aware of the web of Intention, I began a series of drawings I called "the throughline." The drawings were of a human, arms outstretched, head tilted back, face upward towards God. I thought of the drawings as being me, and every human being. The human was being held up and carried along by a stream of energy flowing through her body. All along the stream were the events of her life: loves, loneliness, deaths, celebrations, rage, and laughter. And through it all she surrendered to the power of the stream. Surrendering to the "throughline" means committing to live life fully no matter what happens, and trusting that the Source is interwoven throughout it all.

Reaction vs. Creation

Living with intention is creating each moment as the person you want to be—with the thoughts, words, behavior, and deeds you want to embody. Every moment is a choice. Whether you curse at the driver who cuts you off on the freeway or smile at a child, it's all a choice, a series of daily intentions and choices that sends its message strumming across the web of life. Do your words and actions stem from love or fear?

"Every single thing that we do—from the moment we're born until the moment we die—we can use to help us realize our unity and completeness with all things," writes Pema Chodron. "We can use our lives, in other words, to wake up to the fact that we're not separate: the energy that causes us to live and be whole and awake and alive, is just the energy that creates everything, and we're part of that. We can use our lives to connect with that, or we can use them to become resentful, alienated, resistant, angry, bitter. As always, it's up to us."

Each of the chapters in this book builds on the ones before it. In the last chapter we talked about awareness of ourselves and others—we cannot change or grow until we are aware and observant of our own behavior as well as our relationship to all of creation. In this chapter we considered the ways in which we can begin to act intentionally and decisively based on our awareness.

The poet Rumi talks about our choices and intentions in each moment as if they were animals inhabiting our body in his poem "A Goal Kneels."

The inner being of a human being is a jungle.

Sometimes wolves dominate,

sometimes wild hogs.

Be wary when you breathe!

At one moment gentle generous qualities,

like Josephs, pass from one nature to another.

The next moment vicious qualities move in hidden ways;

Wisdom slips for a while into an ox!

A restless, recalcitrant horse suddenly

becomes obedient and smooth-gaited.

A bear begins to dance.

At each moment you have a choice. You can create a dancing bear rather than a wild hog when you respond to life with creative rather than reactive behavior.

Wake up and grab your paintbrush! Your paintbrush is your mind. Your paintbrush is your intention. What do you intend to create today?

Chapter 3

Fearing the Tigers
Living in the present

Journal Entry 10/18/01

I went to the Great Bodhnath Stupa and did a circular walking meditation with about 200 Tibetans. I walked for almost an hour with the aim of taming my mind and letting go of my ego armor. So much for that. I was so aware of everyone and everything around me. Wizened old faces, smooth-skinned teenagers, some people walking fast, others hobbling with canes, a few in wheelchairs. Mothers with children, novice monks in their scarlet robes, men in business suits. People were singing and chanting, and a few people were even chatting as they walked. I didn't expect meditation to be so noisy! The entrance to the great circle is crowded with village shops and I could hear the clerks, shoppers, and owners calling out to each other, laughing and chattering. There are prayer wheels all around the Stupa and after my meditation I did several walks around, turning each and every wheel. And still, my monkey mind played. Maybe my Western mind just isn't up to the discipline of Eastern enlightenment.

When I first arrived in Nepal, I had days and days on end in the monastery with nothing to do but my meditation and prostration practice. In an effort to "do" rather than just "be" I begin to come up with useful activities rather than just sit in the moment. I'd take a trip down the hill to go to the store, or check my e-mail, clean my bathroom, wash my socks. A cook at the monastery who speaks English sometimes invited me on hikes to abandoned Hindu temples and I would excitedly go—so happy to have something to do!

I learned that without anything to do I become restless and agitated. I create chores and activities to occupy my mind. Where is my stillpoint?

The Blank Moment

The present is the wave that explodes over my head, flinging the air with particles at the height of its breathless unroll; it is the live water and light that bears from undisclosed sources the freshest news, renewed and renewing, world without end.

—Annie Dillard

Annie Dillard is right: life is full of beautiful, stunning, amazing *fresh news from undisclosed sources.* Open your ears and eyes. What is happening right now? Perhaps a child's laughter, a bird's song, a wispy cloud floating across the sky, the face of a loved one smiling at you. Each moment is perfect, complete in itself and will never be seen or heard again in exactly the same way. In another moment, all will be different.

In the West, we have a lot of trouble with just *being*, quietly existing in the stillpoint that T.S. Eliot describes, and content with the present. We usually have to be *doing* something, or, like the girl and boy scouts, ever-prepared for whatever we might need to do. At home we may be thinking about a way to solve a problem at the office. At the office we worry about conflicts at home. In conversation, we rarely ever give our full attention and *listen* to what others are saying to us. We're usually planning what we will say next. We obsess about what happened yesterday, even though we can no longer change it, and worry about what may befall us tomorrow. We are so involved in yesterday and tomorrow that today slips by unnoticed with all its wealth of information, joy, and mystery.

I once practiced meditation at a beautiful retreat center outside of San Francisco. In a sun-bright room with gleaming wooden floors, rays of color streaming through high windows, my mind was everywhere but there. Thinking about my work, planning how I would integrate this experience into my next workbook, even singing Jimi Hendrix's "Purple Haze" at the top of my imaginary lungs. After a while, I found myself thinking about how I would describe this experience to my friend and business partner when I returned home. I saw myself telling him how beautiful this moment was, the room, the sun, the people, the teachers, the entire experience. Then I realized what I was doing. I almost burst out laughing. I wasn't even *in* the experience I was telling him about. I was already back home discussing it.

The Creative Moment

Living in the moment you are completely free. You are a blank canvas in which you are free to be, say, do, think, believe, anything you want. You can determine your life, by not basing your reactions on avoiding discomfort or early childhood programming. Express yourself! Completely and freely. Waking up to Life means you don't have to follow anybody else's patterns or beliefs. You are who you are and you change with each passing moment. Discover your own voice, your own mind, and express it in this moment. Creativity, whether it be writing, painting, cooking or whatever your art, is very much a Buddhist practice. It gives you a chance to step out of your confinement, out of your preconceived notions and ideas, look at the world around you and say, "Why not try it this way?"

Since pure awareness of nowness is the real buddha....
By simply relaxing in this uncontrived, open, and natural state,
We obtain the blessing of aimless self-liberation of whatever arises.
—Dudjom Rinpoche

The psychologist Mihaly Csikszentmihalyi describes the Eastern idea of living completely in the moment as a Western practice called "flow." He compares it to what sports psychologists call "being in the zone," a state of transcendent absorption in which you stretch beyond your former limits and anything becomes possible. In a state of flow, you feel alert, unselfconscious and totally absorbed in the present moment. You are so completely attuned and concentrated on the task at hand that awareness and action become one. Whether writing, painting, climbing a mountain, making love or strumming a guitar, you become unaware of the passage of time, of the past or future, of anything except what is occurring in that moment.

In each precious moment, Life reveals itself to us. As the Western philosopher Franz Kafka put it: "You don't need to leave your room. Remain sitting at your table and listen. Don't even listen, simply wait. Don't even wait. Be quite still and solitary. The world will freely offer itself to you. It has no choice. It will roll in ecstasy at your feet." The Eastern philosopher Lao Tzu saw it the same way:

To the mind that is still, the whole universe surrenders.

Staying firmly rooted in the present moment is not only the most enlightened thing you can do, it is also the healthiest. Says the Buddha:

The Secret of health for both mind and body is not to mourn for the past, not to worry about the future, nor to anticipate troubles, but to live the present moment wisely and earnestly.

When we suspend past and future thinking and dwell in the web of now, we discover that it is made of love.

The Divine Moment

Deepak Chopra writes, "When we are truly present, all we see is love." Teilhard de Chardin believed that "Love is the affinity which links and draws together the elements of the world. Love, in fact, is the agent of universal synthesis." Many Christian theologians understand God's essence as love. Karl Barth wrote, "that he is God—the Godhead of God—consists in the fact that He loves."

When you are completely present, something strange and wonderful happens: you stop being in your head, and your heart opens. The distracting thoughts of worry, guilt, insecurity, things to do, and things not done, disappear and you sink into a state of love. It usually is not Eros or romantic love. It is more of a universal love or reverence for the beauty of all life. Love is the fabric that makes up our entire universe. Just for a moment, give Love a color. Sometimes I see it as a purple web filled with energy. See Love. Imagine how it looks, how it feels, its touch, and its scent. Now that you have made it tangible, see it all around you. See yourself living in it. Live in love.

Living completely in the present, you see everything as Divine. Everything, every person, as the spark of divine that they are. You also embrace your own Divinity. Knowing that you are Love incarnate. You are the body that love flows through. You are the puppet of love. Knowing that you are God's precious one. You are a beautiful essence that has come to bless this planet with your goodness. There is nothing else for you to do.

Why do we resist the present moment?

How many times have I walked into a party and immediately starting jumping to conclusions about how the evening is going to go? I look around, see who is there, make a few associations and judgments. "That guy looks like my old boyfriend. Yuk." "That woman fingering her hair looks boring as hell." "Those people don't look friendly." I head for the bar. A drink usually helps me relax a little. Then, I slowly walk around the room casually nodding and saying polite hellos. I was right, this party is going to be "one of those." I find a few people I know, indulge in a little stale chatter, and leave early. What a waste of an evening! And whose fault is it? It's mine! I am the one who jumped to conclusions. I am the one who closed open doors. I am the one who could not find anything or anyone to celebrate or explore in a room full of people, food, and music. And it was all based on fiction! All based on stories I made up in my head, linked to the past, which weren't even true.

This is typical of how we live life. Like the party, every moment in life is filled with fresh opportunities to create whatever we want. Instead of walking fearlessly into the blank moment clear and clean, most of us take our ideas and baggage from the past and drag it along with us. The past baggage fills up the new moment so completely, there is no room for anything new. We have already decided how we will act in certain situations and what the people we meet are going to be like and how we're going to act toward them. We allow ourselves very little freedom on a day-to-day basis.

We carry the past around, nurse resentments and grudges, or we fear what the future will bring—and that prevents us from seeing the beauty in the present. Every moment lost in worry or regret is a moment lost to joy and beauty.

What keeps you out of the present moment?

Do you obsess about the past by analyzing a conversation with your spouse from two hours or two days ago? Recall embarrassing moments when you were not at your best? Think about a hurtful comment your co-worker spoke to you? Feel guilty over something you have done or said?

Or do you dwell in the future? Feel anxiety about paying next month's bills? Daydream about finding the perfect man or woman? Worry about your job security?

Filling the blank moment with the past or future is a self-protection mechanism. It is a way to live life in a cocoon. It keeps us safe and gives us the illusion of control. It also keeps us blind and asleep. There is an old Inuit saying:

Yesterday is ashes; tomorrow wood.
Only today does the fire burn brightly.

Being *alive* is going into the blank moment without the safety of the past patterns. It is seeing every moment as fresh, new, and exciting. It is not comparing each moment, place, or person with the old. Every man will not treat you this way. Your boss isn't always like this. Your husband doesn't have to respond in this way. If you have acted with anger in a situation in the past, it does not mean you "have to" act with anger in this moment. Because something happened in the past doesn't mean it will repeat itself in the future.

In every moment, you have the opportunity to choose who you are going to be.

Which part of your Self do you want to embody? You may not always be able to shed the comfort of the cocoon. You may make mistakes along the way. Have compassion for yourself. Know that each choice opens up a multitude of new choices. And you will be given many opportunities to spread your fearless wings. That is the wonderful thing about life. Life gives us the opportunity to learn the lessons we need to learn over and over again until we learn them.

Fear of Tigers

There is a Zen story about a woman being chased by tigers. No matter how fast she runs, she can feel their breath on her neck and knows they are gaining on her. She comes to the edge of a cliff and it looks hopeless. Then she sees some vines dangling from the cliff, grabs on to them and lowers herself over the edge. Safe at last! But then she looks down and she sees there are tigers below her as well, waiting for her to lose her grip. She looks up again and sees a mouse gnawing at the vine she is holding. She looks to the right of her and sees a small clump of wild strawberries. She plucks a plump berry and pops it into her mouth, reveling in its sweetness.

This is how we live. There are always tigers below us and above us. We are always at the moment of death or loss. As the old saying goes, "Nobody gets out of this alive." Why are you wasting even one precious moment fearing the tigers rather than enjoying the strawberry? This "strawberry moment" is all you have.

Your tigers may be fearsome. Perhaps you are going to be laid off in two weeks. Maybe your spouse is dying. Perhaps your doctor has just given you bad news about your health. Maybe you are afraid of growing old. Perhaps you had a serious argument with a cherished friend yesterday. Maybe your parents both died when you were young. Maybe you grew up in a household with little money. No matter what your past—how horrible and difficult—no matter what your future—how scary and daunting—you can choose to live in the present moment and savor the big and small joys that are in front of you now.

I am not suggesting that you repress your grief or your anger about things that are happening or have happened in your life. On the contrary, if that is what you are feeling right now, embrace it and make a decision—what do I want to do about this? Cry? Call my friend? Update my resume and ask friends for help finding a job? Eat healthier food? Write a letter to my parents? (Even if I don't send it. Even if they are dead.) Pray to my ancestors for their help and strength? My point is that you should not spend your precious present moments dwelling on things that happened in the past, nor on things that might happen, or even certainly will happen, in the future.

If you are scheduled to be laid off from your job in two weeks, it does no good to sit around worrying about it. In fact, it does great harm to you physically, mentally, and spiritually. The ability to be in the present moment is a gift when we are faced with tigers. Despite the looming threat, we are still able to sit down and blissfully enjoy a thunderstorm, or a fresh baked cookie, or the flowers in the garden. And we are more effective at fighting tigers if and when they do attack if we are fully present. You are more likely to find a new job, or a way to save your current one, if you are completely engaged in your work and your job search.

Even in the midst of tragic, nearly unendurable loss, it is not only possible, but also important to live in the present. A woman I knew whose husband was dying of cancer taught me a lot about finding small joys in the midst of pain and tragedy. She would savor the half hour she had to herself each morning, before her husband, Jim, woke up and her caretaking role began. She would sip her coffee, enjoying the aroma, and the way the cream swirled in it like clouds. She would read the newspaper and be reminded she was not alone in her experience of tragedy. She would enjoy the simple task of rinsing her cup, and then go to her husband and kiss his face to awaken him.

They would often look out the window together, noting the movement of leaves on the walnut tree outside, delighting in the dancing shadows moving on the mowed grass. When he was strong enough, they would go for a short walk together and visit with neighbors who happened to be out. They would play with the neighborhood pets. When she bathed him, she noted every texture and mark on his skin. She would make sure that every inch of him was clean and fresh. Sometimes despair would overcome them and they would cry together: grieving that their remaining time together was short. But it seldom lasted long, because a bird singing outside, or a letter from a friend, or the simple joy of holding hands would divert their attention. They did not repress their grief, and they did not let the knowledge that he was dying rob them of the present.

Similarly, it is possible to live in the present despite a terrible past. In Nepal, I met a gentle forty-year-old monk who was a high teacher called a Khenpo. Like all the other monks, he took pleasure in the simplest activities of everyday life. Khenpo was an incredibly happy man. He had a little dog named Drolma that followed him everywhere. Khenpo didn't speak English, but he was always quick with a smile for me. When he saw me, he would point to something, a beautiful sunset or the antics of Drolma, and he would giggle or laugh. It was infectious—I always laughed with Khenpo, who celebrated his world every day.

One day I watched him as he played and tossed a ball for Drolma, laughing with joy as the little dog frolicked. As he turned, I saw the deep red scar that slashed across his eye and cheek. It was a reminder of his year in a prison camp in Tibet.

When he was a young child, one of eight children, his mother had witnessed five of her children die of starvation due to a famine resulting from the Chinese occupation of Tibet. After Khenpo became a monk, his monastery was raided, and he was taken to a prison camp where he was beaten and made to work at hard labor for a year.

Khenpo never said how he got the scar or talked about his time in prison. Despite all the suffering of his life and of the Tibetan people, he never dwelled on what *was*. Awake and aware in the moment, he drank pleasure from every moment of his everyday world.

Reach for the strawberry. Let the tigers wait.

Another reason some people object to the idea of living in the present is because, after all, *you must plan for the future, or what will become of you?*

What we often fail to see is that we can only create our future if we *live in the present.* The present is where everything is accomplished. All works of great genius have happened in the present moment, with full attention to the task at hand, being "in the flow."

The state of flow in which you expand beyond your previous capabilities can only take place in the present moment.

The many distractions of our busy life also keep us from the present moment. Our minds are so busy and running that we have become a culture of multi-taskers. Driving the car while on the phone. Doing work while watching our child's soccer game. Eating dinner and watching the news. Faster and more.

Multi-tasking keeps you from doing any one thing well. I have found myself talking on the phone to a client and answering e-mail at the same time. I stopped this kind of multi-tasking because I realized that I was not fully attentive to the people involved and not doing the relationships justice.

Whatever we are doing, our minds are usually occupied with useless chatter and inner conversations. Our crazed monkey mind runs off on detours and field trips practicing and planning for things that may never come; going over past events or worrying about something we did or said; replaying arguments to prove to ourselves that we're right and they are wrong. *The past is over and the future may never come.* All you have is this moment. Can you truly be here?

What kind of "field trip" are you going on? Do you really want to go there?

When we get caught up in the busy-ness of the mind, we are not really living. We are really not even in this world. We are in a fantasy world of past and future. The present is the only place we can free ourselves from the faulty belief systems of the past, instead of allowing our hurt child to control our lives. Awareness in the present gives us the power to choose thoughtfully and wisely how we want to respond to people and situations.

Being in the present means that you are one hundred percent present in what you are doing at that moment. If you are driving, you are driving. Period. When you are having a conversation with your child, you are totally with him or her and listening, not talking and looking through the mail, or talking and planning what to do about dinner. When you are answering an e-mail, there is nothing else in your world but that e-mail.

"This very moment is the perfect teacher," writes the American Buddhist nun Pema Chodron. "Awareness is found in our pleasure and our pain, our confusion and our wisdom. It's available in each moment of our weird, unfathomable, ordinary everyday lives."

The poet Rumi described our every moment as a "guest house" in which we have something to learn from every visitor:

This being human is a guest house
Every morning a new arrival.
A joy, a depression, a meanness,
some momentary awareness comes
as an unexpected visitor.
Welcome and entertain them all!
Even if they are a crowd of sorrows,
who violently sweep your house
empty of its furniture,
still treat each guest honorably.
He may be clearing you out for some new delight.
The dark thought, the sham, the malice,
meet them at the door laughing,
and invite them in.
Be grateful for whoever comes,
because each has been sent
as a guide from beyond.

Embracing the power of the blank moment is an exciting way to live. It opens you up to endless possibilities, opportunities, and lessons. It allows you to create your life in every situation with intention. It may feel a little risky at first. New behaviors always are. But when you live in the present without all the past baggage and future fears, you will be amazed how light you feel!

Control your thinking. Don't let your mind control you. When your mind begins to distract you from the present with some new sidetrack, stop and ask yourself, *Is this where I want to go?* If it is, choose it. If it isn't, decide a new direction for yourself. Buddhist philosophy suggests numerous ways to train that little monkey mind.

Training the Monkey

Staying in the present is the simplest and most difficult thing you will ever do. The main method for re-training and quieting the monkey mind is meditation.

The end results of meditation are many. Meditation trains the speed-addicted, restless mind. It has physical benefits such as lowering blood pressure and easing the effects of stress on the body. It diverts the mind's attention from fears of the future and resentments about the past and brings it wholly back into the present. Perhaps most important, it opens the heart to the heaven of love and beauty that only exists in this one, precious, Divine moment.

In a state of meditation, as in a state of flow, the brain emits the slow, rhythmic alpha waves characteristic of a conscious state of relaxed wakefulness.

For most beginning meditators, the simplest way to begin is by using the breath as a focus.

A breathing meditation

Meditation can be as simple as becoming completely aware of and focused on your breathing. The breath is the gateway to the present in this meditation. Sit on a cushion or mat with your legs crossed. If this is uncomfortable or not practical, you can also sit upright on a chair or couch. Keep your spine as straight as possible, and relax your body. As you breathe, feel the air move in and out of your body. Concentrate on your breath. Breathe slowly, deeply, rhythmically, naturally, in and out. Keep your breathing circular, without pausing between inhale and exhale. Concentrate on your breath.

It takes time to train the monkey mind, so don't get impatient. When your thoughts begin to wander (and they will!) just quietly observe your thoughts, then let them go and continue focusing on your breath. If you hear a noise or get an itch, just note it (scratch it if you must!) and return quietly to your breath.

As you breathe, count from one to ten. One as you inhale, two as you exhale, three as you inhale, and four as you exhale, and so on until you reach ten. Then count backwards from ten to one on the next ten breaths. Keep your attention on your breath and the counting. Once again, whenever your mind begins to wander, bring it gently back to breath. You can also repeat one of your new truths or one of the nine attitudes using the phrase as a mantra. Mantra is a Sanskrit word meaning "protector of the mind." Using these statements as a mantra helps anchor down your monkey mind and bring you back from unwanted field trips.

Meditation is a simple technique to help you work with your mind and bring you back to the present. As you become more proficient in this simple technique, you can transfer its stress-reducing benefits to your everyday life. Whenever your mind feels out of control, when you feel caught up in emotions, stress, fear, or anger, simply bring your mind back to your breath and nurture yourself with loving compassion.

You will find that you can do this throughout the day—just a few deep, concentrated breaths will dispel negative emotions and make you more aware of what's going on both inside you and around you. When you have this awareness, you can make powerful choices that are congruent with your highest Self.

Other meditations

The more often you meditate, the easier and more beneficial it will become. There are many ways to meditate. A few good books written on the subject include *How to Meditate: A Guide to Self-Discovery* by Lawrence Leshan; *Miracle of Mindfulness* by Thich Nhat Hanh; and *Wherever You Go, There You Are: Mindfulness Meditation in Everyday Life* by Jon Kabat-Zinn, and there are many others.

There are walking meditations and dance meditations. Meditations can utilize chanting, music, or visualization. In his wonderful book, *Peace Is Every Step,* Thich Nhat Hanh suggests eating meditations, walking meditations, driving meditations. He even suggests this excellent phone meditation:

Buddhist monks use temple bells to remind them to come back to the present moment, writes Thich Nhat Hanh, and you can use the ring of your telephone. Instead of jumping up to answer the phone on the first ring, use the ring as a reminder to take several deep breaths and bring yourself into the present moment. He suggests that "the next time you hear the phone ring, just stay where you are, breathe in and out consciously, smile to yourself, and recite this verse (which monks say when temple bells ring): 'Listen, listen. This wonderful sound brings me back to my true self.'" Answer on the third or fourth ring after you have centered yourself, and you will find you are much more calm and present for the person on the other end of the line.

Anything in which you can remain completely in the present, whether it be gardening or playing an instrument can create a restful, meditative state.

Now Questions

When you find yourself distracted from the present, pause, take a couple of deep breaths and ask yourself the questions listed below. It can also help to write them out in your notebook in the morning to create an intention for the day.

... What am I missing by not being in the present? What have I ignored or missed?

... What pain, fear, or faulty belief system am I medicating?

... If this were the last thing I was to do today, how would I want to do it?

... What do I want to create in this situation?

... Who do I want to be in the next blank moment?

An experiment: Being present with someone you love.

Here is a dual meditation based on the work of David Deida, author of *Intimate Communion* and other books.

Sit facing a friend or loved one. Look into his or her eyes. Begin to match your partner's breath. You are alive, right now. Feel your heart beating in your chest. Soften your belly and relax your jaw. Feel your heart's rhythm radiating outward, pulsing in your hands, face and neck. Silently offer your heartbeat to your companion and to the world. Your heart is beating as an offering to your partner and the world. *You are that offering.*

As you make eye contact with the other person, realize that the way love moves in you is your true destiny. In this moment, allow your breath to be full, strong, and tender as if pressing love from your deep belly into the softness of your companion. Relax your muscles, open your senses, and feel into the world around you, as if feeling into the light of a dream, breathing this light in and out. From your deep heart and soft belly, offer love outward in all directions. That is what you are: an offering of love to the world.

Open your heart more fully now. If you feel a flash of fear, breathe even more deeply in and out. As you inhale, expand your belly more fully, filling your deep gut with love's light and energy. Then, as you exhale, offer love outward to all, relaxing your muscles, feeling out into the colors of the world as you continue breathing. Feel your partner more deeply. Feel their heart's longing and joy as you breathe their aliveness in and out of your heart. Breathe the aliveness of the entire moment in and out. Continue opening, feeling all, breathing all, loving open, allowing your actions to be an offering. When fear or distraction returns, feel its shape. Feel your fear, feel your partner's fear, feel everyone's fear and darkness. Inhale everyone's fear deep into your open heart, remake it into love and exhale love's open light as an offering.

Now, see your partner or friend as one with God. See them as Divine. See them as the manifestation of Love itself. The person who sits in front of you IS Love. The person sitting in front of you IS one with God. Remember that you are the same. You are both made up of the same beautiful energy that is the Divine. Your partner is you and you are both the energy of all that is.

Really look at this beautiful being, this beautiful essence. Say to yourself, "I devote myself to you so that you may live awake and fearless in the world." Feel your heart opening in devotion to God or Love. Imagine yourself kneeling before them, as if a servant humbling offering service. Again, feel the sweetness of your heart as it opens wider and wider. Stay in this place of devotion. Dwell in this place of surrender to Love. Commit your life to it. You are Love, and you live as Love — Gracefully, Divinely in this *Perfect.....Present.....Moment.*

Chapter 4

Flow Like a River
Living with Impermanence

Journal Entry 11/8/01

It has just rained at Wat Pah Nanachat. I have been asked to perform the ritual sweeping of the paths. I'm excited, because I've just arrived and I know the daily "sweeping of the paths" is a long tradition in the forest monasteries.

I sweep. My mind is on my breath. I am very present. Then, I am thinking of friends back home; I am thinking of how beautiful the forest is; I am thinking "What kind of bird song is that?" Back to the breath. I sweep. I breathe.

I begin to take pride in my work. The leaves are moved aside by my sweeps of the broom and there is the simple beauty of the clear forest floor. I sweep. I breathe. I flash back to the awards I received as a child at camp for "Cleanest Room." I will make this the best-looking path in the entire monastery. I will not leave a single leaf on the packed earth of the path. Perhaps the monks will praise my work. Back to the breath. I sweep.

I laugh quietly to myself as I realize that even here—alone on a forest path in a monastery in Thailand—my craving for achievement and recognition is making itself known.

I sweep. I smile. I focus on my work and my breath. I don't notice two big blisters on my hands until later. Finally, I come to the end of the path. I am proud of my work and happy to be here in the forest.

I gaze back along the clean path. It looks beautiful. I turn to walk away and I hear the slight rustling of a breeze through the forest branches. I watch as the trees lining the path sway a little in the wind. And gently...unhurried...a sprinkling of leaves float down to the path. The forest is calm and quiet for a few moments. Then, another small breeze. Another light sprinkling of leaves descends to the forest floor, and a few more come to rest on the path. I smile. I breathe.

Everything changes

The Principle of Impermanence means that nothing stays the same. That is the one guarantee in this life. Every beginning means something has come to an end; every ending is also a starting point. No matter how much we want things to stay the same, things *will* change. You don't have to be a mystic or a scientist to know how fast things change, and how uncertain and impermanent our lives are. Nothing is permanent. What goes up must come down. The forest burns and a meadow emerges. The body ages and the eyes lose focus. The baby grows up and you are a grandparent. The marriage is over and you fall in love. The bank forecloses and you move to a new city. The path is clean, and with a slight wind, covered with leaves again. .

Everything changes, including you.

We are in a constant state of flux. Cells in our bodies are dying and yielding to new ones. Emotions, ideas, and memories flash in and out of our thoughts in each moment. The expressions on our faces change from moment to moment with our moods. You are not the same person you were ten years ago. You are not even the same person you were a few minutes ago.

Impermanence is a key concept in Buddhism. It is one of the three marks of existence. The true nature of existence is that nothing is permanent or stable.

Nothing lasts.

Buddha taught that life is like a river. It is a progression of moments in time, different moments, always changing in a single great flow. The river of yesterday is not the same as the river of today. The river of this moment will be different than the river of the next moment.

The lesson of letting go is one of the hardest we humans must learn. If there is something good in our lives, we want it forever. If there is something bad in our lives, we want it to change and change fast so that we can cling to the next good thing. As the old saying goes, "We want what we can't have, and we don't want what we have."

We resist certain knowledge of impermanence because we are afraid. We cling to the illusion of security in order to avoid anxiety. We want to know what's going to happen, what to expect. We crave a zone of safety, where we are not confused and feel in control of events. Clinging is the action of the child-self who seeks comfort by clutching a favorite blanket or toy when faced with uncertainty.

Not knowing *can* be scary. Ask yourself this question: Do I want to wake up to life's mysteries and realities, or do I want to live and die in fear?

As long as we insist on believing in security—in changelessness—we will ultimately be unhappy. The tighter we hold on, the stronger our grip, the more painful the eventual letting go. When we understand impermanence, we celebrate what is, and we accept when it passes on into something else.

Everything changed when I traveled from Nepal to Thailand. I left the airy spaciousness of a mountaintop for the deep forest of Wat Pah Nanachat, a monastery near Laos and Cambodia. Tan Metikko, a monk who tends to the needs of guests, greeted me. I was given a Kuti, a small hut, surrounded by a graveyard. Toilets and showers were separate structures and shared with other women. At first, Tan gave me a Kuti with no electricity. He thought it would be good for me. Later in the evening he said I could change to the Kuti that had one light bulb if I wanted to. I changed immediately. I slept on the floor on a thin straw mat. I was given the only clothing I could wear, white shirts and long black skirts.

I immediately missed Nepal. My private room, the friendly, laughing Tibetan monks, the colorful rituals, the amazing cooking. But Buddhism is practiced differently in these Thai forest monasteries. In Thailand, there is renunciation, discipline, asceticism. And very little talking—especially to women. They also avoid handing things to women. Tan was the exception, although he had to have another monk present when he was with a woman.

At Wat Pah Nanachat, we ate only one meal a day, and it was prepared from food donated by the local villagers and gathered by the monks on alms rounds each morning. All our practices were to increase mindfulness: bow three times whenever you get up or sit down to bring your attention to what you are doing. Maintain silence most of the time, with an emphasis on watching the thoughts and body. The idea was to tame the chaos of the mind and learn how to control and observe thinking rather than have it control you. Good and valuable practices, but I still missed Nepal.

After only three days, I became mentally whiny. I was way out of my normal comfort zone, and I was suffering. My meditations were interrupted by my bitching, ego-focused mind with multiple complaints:

I want to leave. I'm hungry. It's humid, sticky, hot. I hate these bugs! I don't want to sweep the paths. I'm sick of sleeping on the hard tile floor. I want a massage. I don't want to clean toilets. I'm tired. It's hot. My skin is greasy. Why don't the monks even talk to the women here? They should have Dharma talks or at least acknowledge the lay people more. I should go. I want. I need. I like. I've got to find. I don't like. I'm entitled to. I hope. I expect. Am I good? Will I be good? Look how special I am. Look how spiritual I am. Why do I have to? Look what I can do. Look what I've done. Look how hard I work. Look at these blisters on my hands from sweeping.

Although I had committed to the eight precepts you have to follow at the monastery, including not taking the life of any creature, I was bit by an ant one night in my Kuti and completely lost it. I was a crazed woman, pounding the floor as hard as I could with my shoe. I massacred every ant in sight.

The next morning, I fled the monastery and took a bus to town. I found an Internet café and complained about my suffering to all my friends by e-mail. I called a local spa and a warm-voiced British woman suggested I come stay with them right away. Massages and warm baths beckoned. Other westerners were staying there.

A friend immediately responded by e-mail and pleaded with me to return to the monastery. He said, "I don't have the courage to do what you're doing. It feels like you're doing this for me, too." I thought, "If I can't work with my mind and perceptions here in Thailand, how can I ever do it when I'm triggered by all the distractions at home? Maybe I'll stay the seventeen more days and see what happens." I did, and I am grateful I did. I learned some powerful lessons at Wat Pah Nanachat on death, impermanence, and attachment. The first one was that when we resist change and refuse to learn the lessons of the moment, we allow the "I" to control the experience, and we create our own hell.

Non-Attachment

Impermanence is the reason for the Buddhist philosophy of non-attachment. Some people interpret the idea of non-attachment as renouncing the world, or even choosing poverty as a spiritual path. Or they fear non-attachment means they will lose their "edge," their desires, and their passions.

"Non-attachment is not the elimination of desire," writes Stephen Levine. "It is the spaciousness to allow any quality of mind, any thought or feeling, to arise without closing around it, without eliminating the pure witness of being…" He goes on to say:

"It is an active receptivity to life."

Non-attachment means one simple thing: I recognize a fact of life—everything changes, and I only have this one precious moment for experience, for growth, for discovery. Other words for attachment include: craving, addiction, obsession, rigidity, narrow-mindedness, resistance, compulsion, and misery.

Words to describe non-attachment are: openness, adaptability, creativity, perspective, flow, letting go, yielding, and bliss.

Non-attachment is the path to freedom, while attachment cages our souls and creates hell on earth. Attachment is our insistence that our lives be the way we wish them to be, or the way they were, rather than how they *are* now. It is our resistance to life.

A moment comes, it's not quite how we want it to be, and we resist. We are attached to having it a certain way and so we begin to struggle to control it. We may control it by running into a habit like overeating or control it by judging the situation or the people involved. We can be attached to opinions and ideas, to possessions or relationships, to how we think our spouses or boyfriends or bosses or parents *should* behave (rather than how they actually do).

Lama Surya Das, in his book *Awakening to the Sacred* describes the basic four attachments that do us in:

Attachment to pleasure/pain

Most of us are attached to pleasure—we crave what feels good, looks good, tastes good. We crave chocolate even if it makes us gain weight, and we crave a new car even when we can't afford it. We may drink too much or smoke cigarettes because of their temporary pleasures, even when we know the pleasure is fleeting and the habits harmful to us. Some people are just as addicted to pain as pleasure, and most of us have become attached to pain more than once in our lives. We nurse hurt feelings and resentments, and we indulge in self-pity. As painful as these feelings are, we're still attached to them.

Attachment to opinions and ideas

Our opinions and ideas—our personal view of reality—can cause great stress when they conflict with someone else's personal view. Why do we generally avoid talking about religion, politics, or sex? Because we tend to form very definite opinions in these areas, as well as judgments against people who disagree with us. People with rigid opinions and ideas will often try to browbeat others to get them to agree with their confirmed beliefs. Such browbeating can break up a marriage, or start a war.

Attachment to Rites and Rituals

This attachment is to forms rather than substance. We can get caught up in religious rituals, diet rituals, cleaning rituals, all kinds of behavior rituals. None of these activities are "bad," it's just that we need to recognize the reason for the behavior and achieve some balance. Surya Das tells of a woman who spent so many hours of the day on spiritual regimens like meditation, yoga, and shopping for her vegetarian diet that she had no time left to form friendships or personal relationships. Buddhism has its rituals, but Buddha did not teach obsessive observance of ritual at the expense of simply being awake and aware.

Attachment to Ego

This is the part of Buddhist philosophy that gives many people pause. Perhaps our strongest attachment is to our own ego. "This is who I am." For most of us, self-preoccupation is the main theme of our lives. Attachment to our own sense of self can lead us to feelings of "better than," "smarter than," "better looking than" and cut us off from other human beings and life as a whole. We are not Superman or Superwoman, we are simply human, and we share our vulnerable and beautiful human qualities with every other being on the planet.

All attachments are a way we attempt to protect ourselves from pain. Ironically it is our attachments that cause us the most pain.

Walt Whitman advises us: "Argue not concerning God, have patience and indulgence towards the people...re-examine all you have been told at school or church or in any book, dismiss what insults your very soul, and your very flesh shall become a great poem." That's non-attachment.

Change happens. Waking up to this fact means being able to go with the flow. Accepting change means allowing life to follow its crazy course without becoming discouraged and weakened because you are trying to hold on to what is gone. How do you deal with small changes in your life? How do you deal with big ones? Your life is moving like a rapid river towards the ocean. Do you ride the boat with joy and trust? Or are you rowing as hard as you can against the current?

Life is brief

Life is *very* brief. You may live another thirty, forty or fifty years, or you may live only another day, week, or month. You could get in your car to run an errand, get struck by a drunk driver and be gone ten minutes from now.

A major consideration in Buddhist teaching is the hour of death and regrets you may experience about your life. At the moment of death, your precious time is gone, and even if you have lived your life "asleep at the wheel," you cannot go back and change it. The material things you have accumulated in life are no longer of any use to you. Even a billionaire cannot take one mouthful of food, one piece of clothing, or one silver dollar past death's doorstep.

It is sobering to contemplate our own deaths, but only by recognizing death can we learn to live. How will you feel about your life when you look back at it? Did you have a successful career but never really get to know your spouse? Did you love and listen to your children? Did you celebrate life's loves and joys? Spend time with those you love? See the preciousness of each moment?

Death is the great teacher

If you knew you were about to die, and you had the opportunity to call a loved one, what would you say?

On September 11, 2001, many people trapped in the Twin Towers had such an opportunity. During the final minutes of their lives many of these people reached out to their loved ones using cell phones and e-mail. A chef called and left a message for his wife: "I love you. No matter what happens. I love you."

If you had one hour to live, whom would you call? What would you say?

What are you waiting for?

You may not have the luxury of knowing when you are going to die or being able to make a phone call before you do. The truth is, you are dying right now, and you have been every moment since your birth.

The awareness of death is the giver of a meaningful life. This is in no way a "morbid" practice. It is a call to life: A call to live life with as much passion, joy, and awareness as humanly possible. The knowledge of death creates a passion for life— for living your life *now!*

I attended the funeral of a twenty-one-year-old girl in Thailand. Funerals are not usually sad events because Buddhists accept the impermanence of life and its natural cycle. More sadness was present at this funeral because she died so young of AIDS.

At the village cremation site, a pyre was constructed with wood and flammable materials at the bottom. The girl's clothing and personal effects were laid on top of the wood, and at the top of the pyre sat a light, wood coffin containing her remains. Everyone present was given matches, and we paid our respects and said our final farewells as we tossed a match onto the flames.

The monks asked me to be very close to the flames, to watch the body burn. I did so for several hours, meditating on her death by saying, "This is my body. These are my hands, my head. This is my skin, my weight, my hair, all the things to which I am attached." The point of this death meditation is to learn not be attached to form. It is to know that everything changes, and you will be on that bier soon enough. It is to truly understand that

you are not a body.

After the cremation, when all that was left were ashes and shards of bone, the remains were put in a pottery urn and kept within the monastery walls for a brief time. Then the urn was buried in the graveyard in the midst of which my little hut sat.

Do you find it grisly or depressing to think about death, and particularly your own death? The point of "learning how to die," as the monks taught me, is to learn how to live.

The One Thing You Can Count On

In this world of impermanence there is one glue that binds our lives and fills what we would otherwise only experience as emptiness. The essence of our lives—whether you call it Love, the Divine, or God, is the one permanent and encompassing reality you can count on in this life. The only thing that breathes with you through every breath.

When I was in Nepal, I was given the name Choyin Drolma. It means "emptiness which at its essence is love." The emptiness is our openness and acceptance of what is, even as we see it changing before our eyes. We do not need to grasp onto things that are changing in the ephemeral world when we realize our only reality is Love. It is the water we swim in, the air we breathe, the space between and within our atoms, the essence that permeates our ever-changing lives.

When you live with knowledge of impermanence, as well as the reality of Love, you realize how very precious is each and every moment. "Here today, gone tomorrow," is not just a popular saying, it's an inescapable truth.

How amazing is this moment! Every single moment is its own unique gift. If you could take a snapshot of every moment of your life, what a story it would tell. I sometimes think of old black and white pictures that capture a moment frozen in time: a woman studying the lines in her face in the mirror; lovers crossing the street; a child's winning smile.

There is not a single moment in your life that is not magic.

Not one. No matter how mundane or ordinary they seem. Can you appreciate the gift of <u>this</u> moment? It is easy to appreciate a beautiful sunset, a happy, laughing child, the good-bye kiss of a lover at the airport. But can you appreciate the mundane things and even the moments of suffering? Can you find the beauty in balancing your checkbook, driving in traffic, pulling weeds, waiting in the doctor's office, having the flu, a colicky baby, or a lover ending your relationship? Running naked means letting go of the barriers between you and the moment—whether the moment is happy or sad, monumental or mundane.

Try this exercise: the next time you drive to work, notice and appreciate the moments in your car. Experience the weather; notice the people in the cars around you and send them blessings as your traveling companions; appreciate the fact that you can see, move, and know how to drive. Say to yourself, "I appreciate _____." See how many things you can come up with to fill in that blank. "I appreciate my car is working. I appreciate the heater in my seat. I appreciate my sunglasses. I appreciate that my stomach is full. I appreciate that I am running on time." Give this exercise a try with several of your mundane tasks like paying bills, making dinner, mowing the lawn. Working your "appreciation muscle" is a beautiful way of getting out of numbness and getting into gratitude.

One day I had lunch with a business partner. We sat at an outdoor table at the same Chinese restaurant where we dined at least three times a week. We were chatting about work and recent movies when a man walked by. He was apparently homeless, disheveled, yet his eyes were smiling and kind. He was wearing curly brown fur shoes that looked like he was wearing a poodle on each foot. Just at the same moment, a VW Beetle drove by, painted as an advertisement for Jelly Belly. Brightly colored jelly beans covered its exterior. Our conversation stopped, and for a brief moment time stood still. We smiled and sat silently watching the magnificent spectacle that is this life. Magic is all around you. It becomes special when *you* recognize its sweetness and beauty.

"God is our refuge and strength. A very present help in trouble.
Therefore we will not fear though the earth should change, and
though the mountains slip into the heart of the sea; .....
The Lord is with us."
—Psalm 46

Chapter 5

No One is Watching
Living in Integrity

Journal Entry

Upon arrival at Wat Pah Nanchat, I was given a list of requirements that I had to commit to while staying at the monastery. The agreements that I signed on to are strict, and some of them are frankly irritating.

I must wear a uniform consisting of a white top and long black skirt. No jewelry, makeup or any adornment. These particular rules I don't mind much—in fact, they are liberating in their way. I don't have to worry about what to wear (Is it appropriate? Do I look good in this top?). No make-up? No problem. No adornment isn't a big deal either, though I feel naked without earrings in my pierced lobes.

No listening to music (it's not that the monks think music is bad, it's just to prevent any distractions while we are here).

No big deal. I can do without my Walkman for a couple weeks.

No killing of any living creature. Well, the universe and two dozen dead ants know how I did with that one.

And the most annoying rules: women must hold their hands in the namaste mudra prayer position when greeting monks (who are all male), and the woman's eyes must be kept lower than the monk's eyes. Since I'm only five feet tall, the latter isn't a problem for me, but I feel a vague resentment about both requirements. If these monks have so much trouble being chaste that they can't even have a woman look at them during a conversation, maybe they should start a sex-addict counseling group here. And why must I show them respect by approaching them with my hands in prayer position, but they are not required to return this show of respect? I am sorely tempted to flaunt these rules . but I don't. I did choose this experience, and this is part of it.

Oh, also, women must agree to avoid conversing with men at the monastery unless it has to do with chores or the affairs of the monastery. I'm a talker. I'm a curious and sincerely interested talker. This one'll be tough to keep up.

I haven't been here long but I am already learning a lot about myself by noticing which agreements I resist and which agreements I gladly accept.

When you leave this life, you take nothing of the material world with you. Not that fun car you love to drive, not those heirloom ruby earrings you love to wear, not even the clothes you're wearing when they bury, cremate or otherwise dispose of your body. Everything stays here. Yes, you get to write a will and leave the sports car to your favorite charity and the earrings to your favorite niece, and hopefully, you will be remembered for your generosity and thoughtfulness. But you'll also be remembered, by everyone who knew you, for the steadfastness of your integrity, or the lack thereof. The word "integrity" comes from the Latin root word "integer," meaning "whole." Your integrity is your wholeness, and it is more important than anything you can own or buy or leave someone in a will. It is a gift for you and the world—a legacy as well as a current creation and responsibility.

When the word integrity is applied to objects, it refers to the wholeness or purity of a thing. A building has integrity when it is intact and without structural flaws. A wilderness region has integrity when it remains whole and pure without being corrupted by development.

You are whole when what you think, what you say, and what you do are in harmony with your core values.

Integrity—your wholeness—can also be called your ethics or morals, or your value system. Integrated, ethical behavior is described in the Noble Eight-Fold Path of Buddhism as Right Speech and Right Action.

In integrity, we find relief from conflicting emotions and desires. When faced with a decision, instead of being compulsive or impulsive, we ask ourselves: What is the ethical thing to do? What is the action that is most congruent to who we are? This approach demands that we look at the world and ourselves as a whole or in a holistic manner. How will what I do affect the best interests of all involved, as well as my own integrity and self-worth?

When we act with integrity, our life is in "flow." It seems to move along effortlessly, and our body feels light. Living with integrity has a ripple effect on your entire life. It has positive effects on your personal relationships, your work, and even your health.

Here's a little experiment. Think of a time when you did something based entirely on your values—perhaps you stood up for someone who was being unjustly treated or took an unpopular action because you believed it to be for the greater good. Relive that incident in as much detail as possible. Who were the other people involved? What did you do or say? How did it feel before, during, and after the experience? If you are like most people, these are some of the most satisfying experiences in your life.

Now, think of a time when you were not living in integrity. It might have been a time you said "yes," when you knew "no" was the best answer, or a time you didn't tell the whole truth or did something else against your personal belief system. Really feel that experience in all of its fullness. What happened? Who was involved? How did your body feel before, during, and after? How does your body feel now simply remembering the experience?

I remember a time when I was dating a man who I knew wasn't right for me. But the relationship was comfortable and nice. He was kind, generous, and we had a good time together. Still, after a short time, I began to feel restless. Little things he did irritated me—like the way he chewed his food, or the corny compliments he'd say to the waitress. I began to close my heart to him and disconnect from our conversations. I realized I wanted to break up with him. But he was so nice and good to me! I hid the truth and tried to make it work. I began to feel tired and irritable when I was with him, and even a little bit ill at times. It was as if not living my truth was slowly poisoning me.

After ending our romantic relationship, I realized that staying in a relationship that wasn't right for me, I was re-inforcing the belief system, "I'm not good enough to attract the man I really want." I found that after we separated, I had more energy, and I felt hopeful about life and my future. That's what living in integrity and speaking your truth does. Staying in a relationship that isn't working for you is just one example of letting yourself down; you might fail yourself by staying in a job you hate, or holding back forgiveness toward someone who has hurt you.

Living without integrity is one of the most destructive things we can do to ourselves. It can actually make us sick in soul and body. Remember the feelings you had in your body by simply remembering the lack of integrity experience. Now, think of having those feelings all or most of the time. Not being who we are and who we want to be actually leads to disease in the body. Dis-ease—the opposite of ease and effortlessness.

You can use your body as a barometer of your integrity.

Learn to read your body's signals. Anytime you feel dis-ease in your body about an interaction or decision, ask yourself, "Am I living true to who I am and who I want to be?" It can be helpful to write about it in your notebook, using the simple diagram on the following page.

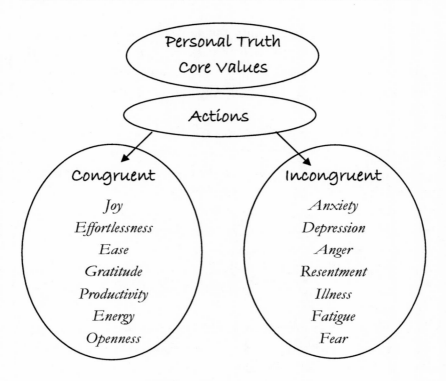

In the first circle, describe your core value—what you most wish to express in this particular instance. What is really important to you? What is in the core of your being? What is your highest personal truth?

In the second circle, describe your actions. What do you show to the outside world? What do others see?

It's easy to recognize whether you are being congruent or incongruent with your true Self, based on the feelings that result. Actions incongruent to your core values lead to anxiety, depression, anger, resentment, sickness, fatigue and fear. Incongruent behavior leads to dis-ease.

Actions congruent to your core values result in joy, effortlessness, ease, gratitude, productivity, energy and openness. It seems simple because it is! Act congruent with who you are and your whole life moves with ease, like the flow of an immense, energetic river.

What are your Values?

What core value did you write in your first circle? It can help to examine and evaluate your values in writing so that you can recognize them in action. Often what we think of as core values are actually based on a faulty belief system, which will also lead to dis-ease when we try to act based on these beliefs. Faulty belief systems lead us to equivocate or qualify our highest values. Here are a few examples of faulty belief systems and core values that might be associated with them. These belief systems are all reflected from the core idea that "I am not OK":

... *Greed* "If I have more, I will feel better."

... *Power* "When I am powerful, people will respect me."

... *Competition* "There is not enough for everyone."

... *Appearance* "I must look young to be attractive."

... *Strength* "No crying is a sign of a strong man."

... *Prejudice* "My religion is better than any other."

... *Lust* "I am only okay when sexually desired."

If you aspire to truth as one of your core values, and yet you believe that you should sometimes lie to stay out of trouble, your actions will result in dis-ease rather than joy. Or if love is one of your highest values, but you condition it with a desperate plea to your partner to "Please never leave me," your actions are based on a faulty belief system about the nature of love (and your own worthiness of receiving it).

Our highest values can be expressed in action in many different ways depending on our belief systems. It has been said that one man's determination is another man's obstinacy. And so it becomes important to not only name a value as important to us, but to also observe and study how this value plays out in our actions.

What is so important to you that you consider its principles essential to your life? Here is a list of values. Consider these and any other core values that occur to you. Look at each one carefully and ask yourself, "How important is this in my life? Does this thing or quality make my life richer? Fill it with more joy? Help me feel true to who I am as a person? Or has this value ever caused me to act in a way that left me feeling ill at ease with myself?"

In your notebook, create your own "Top Ten List" of your core values. Then, narrow that down to your five most important values to live by.

Honesty	**Spirituality**	**Success**
Keeping your word	**Love**	**Accomplishment**
Telling the truth	**Companionship**	**Notoriety**
Family	**Compassion**	**Stability**
Money	**Service**	**Comfort**
Hard work	**Openness**	**Freedom**
Play		

Walking your Talk

Now that you have narrowed your Top Ten Values list to an essential Basic Five, the next question is: Are you living them? Living in integrity means you walk your talk at all times. No halfway here. This is referred to as Right Action in the Noble Eight-Fold Path. Your actions as well as your beliefs and thoughts are daily creating or changing the essential "you" as well as the world you live in.

Are you creating harmony, honesty, kindness, generosity, openness, love? Do you live the values you listed above? Or do you say you value certain things yet give your time and energy to others? Living your values is extremely difficult at times, especially when the world seems to support very different values than your own.

I have heard it said that your level of integrity can be seen in what you do when no one is watching. What "little" things will you do if there is no danger of others' knowing? Do you cheat on your taxes? What if you get more change than you are due at a store? For one week, observe your own behavior closely to see if you are walking the talk. This exercise is not about judging yourself, but simply about noticing your behavior when no one is looking over your shoulder. Awareness of what you are doing, as we discussed in Chapter One, is not judgmental. Rather it is a tool to help you modify your behavior. After becoming aware of your actions, write in your notebook how you feel when you are congruent with your values, as well as how you feel when you are not.

Everything you do speaks volumes about you. In every moment you are sending a message to the world with your thoughts, words, and actions. It's as if you are "branding" yourself with every step. Many corporations invest millions of dollars in branding their businesses. They know that every product they put out, every commercial, every experience a customer has with their company affects that customer's impressions. It is no different for you. Every thing you do makes a statement about who you are. These statements ripple into the web of your life. Throughout the day, stop and ask yourself, "Does what I am saying and doing represent who I am?" "Is this the 'brand' I want to express to the world?"

Your Words

The words you speak are never meaningless—every word out of your mouth *matters*. Words can be creative or destructive, blessings or curses, kind or cruel, gifts or weapons. Your words speak volumes about who you are and how you regard others. We often forget the singular importance of words. Which would you rather hear?

A voice lifted in prayer or song
Words of kindness and compassion
Gentle words spoken softly with a smile

Or harsh lies, raspy, angry voices, cruel gossip? Which words do you speak every day?

Critical to the idea of integrity and right speech is keeping your word. Do others trust you? Do they believe what you tell them? Do you trust yourself?

Keeping your word dictates whether your life runs smoothly, with only minor hitches, or if you live on a roller coaster of promises broken or forgotten, half-truths and alibis.

When you keep your word, your work goes well. Friendships and relationships grow and expand. Even your finances seem to blossom.

Actually there is nothing small in keeping your word. Your word is simply that—your word. Do you do what you *say* you are going to do, when you *say* you are going to do it? Being on time is not any less of a commitment than wedding vows. They are equally weighted on the scale of integrity. Do you return phone calls "tomorrow" when you say, "I'll call you tomorrow"? Do you follow through on your promises or do you constantly give excuses about how busy you are?

I realized the importance of keeping my word after a few weeks at Wat Pah Nanachat in Thailand. Tan Metikko called me into the monastery and said, "It has been brought to my attention that you are conversing too much with the monks." I felt humiliated, like a child being called before the principal, and I burst into tears.

Tan was calm and comforting. He didn't scold me, he just reminded me that limited conversation with the monks was part of the original agreement when I came to stay, and he wanted to be sure that I was aware of what I had agreed to.

"But I don't remember that being in the agreement," I said.

I left in a flurry of emotions. Who had tattled on me to Tan? Did this mean they didn't like me any more or disapproved of me? Would they ask me to leave? Had Tan found out about the ant massacre?

Then I began justifying my behavior. There were so many monks from all over the world at the monastery—England, South Africa, America. I was fascinated by their stories and wanted to know more about why they had journeyed to

Thailand and decided to become monks. It wasn't as if I was trying to seduce them—I was just talking to them! After all, what is the big deal about talking to men? This isn't the Middle Ages and why couldn't I talk to anyone I wanted to? And where did it say that in the agreement, anyway? I didn't remember anything that specific!

I stalked back to my kuti and read the agreement papers with a lawyer's eye for loopholes. Anxiety, anger, fear, insecurity, and resentment began their familiar tap dance in my brain. Despite all the time I had spent lately, learning to be authentic and present and intentional, I fell back into my old bad habits very quickly during this little crisis.

When I re-read the agreement, I found it was very specific about not conversing with monks or laymen at the monastery. It was there in stark black and white in front of my eyes, no wiggle room. I had read it and agreed to it, and then conveniently forgotten it. I only remembered what I wanted to remember about the agreement.

My feelings about the fairness or necessity of the rule were beside the point. I had freely given my word not to indulge in extensive conversations with the men who lived at the monastery. These men had renounced worldly goods and sensuality. This was their lifestyle, and I was their guest and had agreed to their terms of staying at the monastery.

When I broke this agreement, I was very quick to blame someone else rather than examine my own integrity. It's very easy and very convenient to "forget" when we have given our word. I've done it, and I've observed it many times in workshops and personal interactions with others.

How much of your life consists of commitments not kept, or not even remembered?

Keeping your word goes beyond keeping commitments to others. More importantly, it's about keeping commitments to yourself. "To thine own self be true," wrote Shakespeare, "and it must follow, as the night the day, Thou cannot then be false to any man."

Unless we can be true to ourselves first, we cannot be true to others. Being true to your values is one way of keeping your word to yourself. Not lying to yourself. Being awake and aware of the words you speak to yourself. Being true to yourself requires a courageous commitment to truth.

Self-betrayal happens when we refuse to respect our own truth because of fear of how others may react. For example, a woman may be afraid to disagree with her husband because she is afraid he will leave her if she stands up for herself. She may also participate in office gossip even though she thinks it wrong, because she's afraid that her co-workers will reject her if she doesn't join in. This woman is allowing her fears of abandonment to persuade her to be disloyal to herself. She will probably also be over-extended, and do things she doesn't want to do because of her faulty belief system and refusal to speak her own truth. This scared woman doesn't realize that saying "no" will actually result in more respect from others and less stress for herself. The sad thing about self-betrayal is it always backfires and leads to anger and unfinished business.

How do you betray yourself?

When you betray yourself, there are always consequences. Anger can build until you express it in passive-aggressive behavior, a guilt trip, or an out-and-out explosion. Or you may turn your anger inward and become depressed.

When you are angry and depressed, ask yourself specifically, "What am I angry about?" Write down your true reasons for your anger. You may be surprised at the answers. Do you feel angry with yourself for betraying your own values, or do you feel someone else has betrayed you? Once you find your answer, don't just stuff it back down inside, do something about it!

Expressing yourself is one way to right the self-betrayal within you. Write your feelings in your journal or confide in a friend. If you feel you have a legitimate beef with someone else, express your feelings to him or her directly, as calmly and constructively as possible.

Always keeping your word does not mean that you never change your mind or need to change plans. What it does mean is *re-negotiating* your agreement with the other party involved, even if it is yourself. A re-negotiation is just that. It is going to the other person, sharing your feelings and needs, and being open to feedback. This doesn't have to be a long, drawn-out process. It can be as simple as calling a friend to move your lunch forward to 12:30 instead of simply showing up late. It can also be as complex as renegotiating a marital commitment that isn't working any longer. When life changes the circumstances of your agreement, re-negotiate, don't just break your commitment.

Most conflicts in our world, from war and infidelity to

business scams and traffic fatalities, start with people breaking their word.

What if someone offered you a million dollars to keep all of your agreements for one week? Would you do it? Could you do it? Do you remember all the "little" things you have agreed to? Will you honor your larger commitments? My guess is that most of us would fail at this challenge within one day. I can't offer you a million dollars, but I can promise you the joyful ease that comes from living your life with integrity if you keep your word.

Taking Responsibility

You are the creator of your life. Everything in it. Some of you are already arguing "But I didn't create that car accident; the guy just hit me," or "My husband had an affair, it wasn't my fault." Living with integrity means taking responsibility for your part in all that occurs in your life.

Responsibility isn't the same as blame, however. You are not blaming yourself for someone else's mistakes: You are taking responsibility for your own actions and your *response* to the event. Responsibility is Power.

You are not a victim. I am always impressed when people in horrible situations are able to find meaning, purpose, and even gratitude in their lives. Imagine that, gratitude about being in a wheelchair or imprisoned or dying of cancer! That's what responsibility is all about. It's about finding the gift in every moment. Not about whining, complaining, and saying "Why me?—Why am I stuck in this job, this relationship, or this situation?"

Commit now to look at every experience as your opportunity for greatness.

What if every event that felt uncomfortable to you was actually a messenger helping you heal a wound from your childhood? What if every "up-set" was actually a "set-up" from the universe to help you become your highest self? The ultimate assumption of responsibility in your life is accepting that the person, place, or thing that has triggered you is simply the result of a wound within you. Feel that wound. See what the message is for you in the event. Is it *I'm hurt, I don't feel heard,* or *I'm not enough?* to name a few. Go inside and love yourself through your pain. Don't look for external fixes to numb your discomfort. Go inside and heal yourself with forgiveness and compassion. That is the only way true healing can happen. An external band-aid can never heal your internal wounds.

You have the power to create your life with your thoughts, actions, choices, perceptions, and beliefs. Give up the blame game. Give up even talking about what someone did to you.

You are responsible for every action you take. That is the meaning of karma—a simple law of cause and effect. For every action, there is a reaction. Every action you take leads to a reaction from someone or something, which leads to your next action and so on and so on.

No action or word is meaningless or without consequence. In every moment you have a choice of what you want to create. Life is one long string of energy reaching from the beginnings of time to the distant future. Modern science tells us that the simple act of throwing a pebble into a pond will create ripples that eventually become vibrations that will continue throughout infinity.

You are creating your world and your karma right now by your words and deeds and thoughts. Are your ripples screaming "My word always manifests as truth?" or, "My word cannot be counted on, don't believe me." Look at everything you say carefully. What ripples are you creating?

> *I know this now.*
>
> *Every man gives his life for what he believes.*
>
> *Every woman gives her life for what she believes.*
>
> *Sometimes people believe in little or nothing yet they give their lives to that little or nothing.*
>
> *One life is all we have and we live it as we believe in living it.*
>
> *And then it is gone.*
>
> *But to sacrifice what you are and live without belief, that's more terrible than dying.*

—Joan of Arc

Chapter 6

The Joy of Honeybees
Living with Purpose

Journal Entry

I almost left Wat Pah Nanachat when it got too difficult. By staying, I have found that there comes a time when all the chatter of the brain stops. All the complaining. All the "making a case" to support my critical views. All the judging of others to avoid looking at myself. The monks and the people of the small Thai village of Bung Wai are amazing—totally committed to the spiritual life. The fact is, part of my judgment about this place was the thought that I could never have the courage to do what they are doing.

There is a reason for your existence. And it's not simply to provide for your family, or finally buy the house you've always wanted. There is a Divine Purpose for your life. Your soul's purpose in life is the gift that you, and you alone, are here to give. You may not know what your purpose is right now, but nevertheless, you have one. The World needs **you**. It needs your uniqueness—your inner music, your beauty, your hidden talent, your enthusiasm. Every event in your life has molded you and drawn you towards giving what only you can give the world.

Just as a honeybee knows it is born to make honey and possesses the necessary traits to do so, so do you already possess the innate talents to fulfill your purpose.

> *Your purpose can be discovered in your interests, passions, and curiosities.*

Whatever your purpose may be, you will find it to be a source of joy. Expressing your purpose will fill you with enthusiasm. The word "enthusiasm" comes from the Greek, meaning "filled with God." Your Purpose is Divine.

Says the Brazilian writer Paulo Coelho in *Confessions of a Pilgrim*, "I learned the most important lesson of my life: that the extraordinary is not the birthright of a chosen and privileged few, but of all people, even the humblest. That is my one certainty: we are all the manifestation of the divinity of God."

Purpose is woven into the web of your work, your family, your dreams, your trip to the grocery store, your merging into traffic on the freeway—your entire life. You can live your purpose whether you are rich or poor, sick or healthy, in possession of your full physical capabilities, or are handicapped.

Too often we lose sight of our purpose. Caught up in the money game, and determined to acquire all the "toys" of life, we live our lives from want to want, without ever stopping long enough to ask ourselves "what for?" We live in a state of Samsara.

Samsara is a Sanskrit word that literally means perpetual wandering. It describes living an unawakened life—a life held hostage by the needs, wants, and desires of the self. A shipwreck of compulsions, fears, anxieties, doubts. Samsara creates the suffering of daily existence. Samsara is the land of the walking dead.

The most common example of Samsara in our society is the money-driven life. The constant need for more—more money, more stuff, *more*. In Buddhism they call someone caught up in a wanting existence, the "hungry ghost." The hungry ghost has a big belly, a little pinhole mouth and a needle-thin throat. His hunger is insatiable, because no matter how hard he tries to fill up his belly, he can never get enough food through that tiny mouth and narrow throat.

There is only one way out of Samsara, and that is enlightenment—waking up.

Living your full purpose in this life is a big step out of Samsara. Life simply makes more sense. It doesn't mean you don't feel hurt, sadness, or grief. In fact, you experience all the emotions of life more keenly: the easy ones and the difficult ones. When you have purpose, you have the ability to experience life even more fully because you live from a place of stability and strength rather than a place of desperation and fear. Your purpose gives you courage to live your life no matter what happens. Relationships can end, jobs can be lost, people move and change, but when you have purpose you journey through life with courage and joy.

Even in a purpose-filled life, there is still drudgery, pain, and anger. Purpose does not eliminate suffering, it gives meaning to suffering. Victor Frankl in his treasure of a book, "Man's

Search for Meaning," writes, "When man knows the why, he can endure the how." Frankl's book introduced a new form of psychotherapy based upon meaning and purpose as being the motivational force in human life. He created this therapy after enduring years of horror in the Nazi death camps.

Living on purpose contains much suffering and real sacrifice. It is the road less traveled in a world of addiction, escapism, and materialism. Even the monks at Wat Pah Nanachat often missed their families, still worked through past longings of having a family and children, and missed listening to their favorite music.

Cherish your visions. Cherish your ideals. Cherish the music that stirs in your heart, the beauty that forms in your mind, the loveliness that drapes your purest thoughts, for out of them will grow all delightful conditions, all heavenly environment; of these, if you but remain true to them, your world will at last be built.

—*James Allen*

What Purpose Is Not

Whatever your purpose may be, you will find joy in it, not drudgery. Purpose is the reason you exist, not just another item on your "to-do" list.

Rumi describes purpose in life as a Divinely-assigned task. "All things are assigned a task," he writes. "The heavens send rain and light for the herbs of the field to germinate and spring into life. The earth receives the seeds and bears fruit, it accepts and reveals a hundred thousand marvels too numerous to tell. The mountains give forth mines of gold and silver."

So do you have a uniquely assigned, Divine Purpose in life? If you spend your days on a hundred tasks and projects, but accomplish nothing related to your Purpose, you have just wasted your day. "It is just as if a king sent you to the country to carry out a specific task," writes Rumi. "If you go and accomplish a hundred other tasks, but do not perform that particular task, then it is as though you performed nothing at all. So, everyone comes into this world for a particular task, and that is their purpose. If they do not perform it, then they will have done nothing."

Purpose is also not a goal. Goals are important. They are the stepping stones on the path of your life. Your purpose is something much deeper than that. It is the destination those stones are guiding you toward and the material each one is made of.

Your purpose is not about making money or attaining fame. That may happen in the course of fulfilling your purpose. Those who have acquired the outer trappings of success often say they are doing what they born to do, fulfilling their dreams and their own nature. Money was a by-product, not the original goal. John D. Rockefeller said, "The man who starts out simply with the idea of getting rich won't succeed; we must have a larger ambition."

Purpose in Your Work

Do you wake each morning excited to begin work? Or do you dread facing the day? If you are just in it for the paycheck, work can be grueling.

We all want to find work we love that is a reflection of our true purpose. In Buddhism, this relates to the idea of "Right

Livelihood." Simply put, it means work that benefits others rather than harming, exploiting, or abusing them. At the very least, as the Hippocratic oath suggests, you should "do no harm."

In her book *Do What You Love, The Money Will Follow: Discovering Your Right Livelihood* Marsha Sinetar says that work provides you with a way of dedicating yourself to life. Fulfilling your purpose through your work makes that work joyous and playful. "We can start to work so as to create and express something whole, distinctive, beautiful, truthful, and positive," says Sinetar. Kahlil Gibran writes:

"Work is love made visible."

Working at what you love to do, expressing your true purpose in life, you take part in the world; give it your gifts and your love. You will naturally make the world a better place when you work with purpose and heart.

Your purpose is unique to you, and so you are a distinctive piece of the "puzzle" here on earth. Your purpose can be expressed in almost any job or profession, if you think of it as your gift to the world.

"I don't think it helps anyone to get too judgmental about different occupations," says Lama Surya Das in his book *Awakening the Buddha Within.* "Some may say that a doctor or nurse is more helpful to humanity than a banker or mortgage broker, but who knows? An impeccable businessperson can do a lot of good." Although the legal profession is often maligned and made the subject of jokes, we would do well to remember that Abraham Lincoln was a lawyer. So was Gandhi.

We all need each other in our unique purposes — our unique reasons for being.

A woman who loves words becomes a poet. A man who has a natural gift for fixing and repairing becomes a plumber. One day the poet needs a plumber. How wonderful it is if the man who arrives at her door works excellently, honestly, and with a smile. The plumber sometimes needs a poet for words of beauty and inspiration. All our talents and skills fit together in a dazzling, interwoven pattern. The world needs what you, and you alone, have to give.

The poet Pablo Neruda described the joy of finding his purpose in his work:

> *...And something ignited in my soul,*
> *fever or unremembered wings.*
> *And I went my own way,*
> *deciphering*
> *that burning fire....*
> *and suddenly I saw*
> *the heavens*
> *unfastened*
> *and open.*

What is your purpose in work and in your life? Why are you here? What will you leave behind when you're gone? What is your legacy?

In your notebook, write down three words that you would want people to use to describe you after you die—adjectives such as warm, witty, open, loving, passionate. What three words would you want to hear spoken at your funeral? How can you live these words in your work?

What if you want to live your Purpose, but it has been buried under so many layers of the demands of daily life that you don't really know what it is? There are many ways to explore and discover your own unique reason for being.

Exploring the Past

One way to get in touch with your purpose is to examine the past. It is quite common for purpose to be connected to your natural gifts—the talents and interests with which you were born. Think back to when you were a kid. How would you describe yourself when you were young? What talents, skills or activities came naturally for you? What did you most enjoy studying? What did you most enjoy doing in your leisure time? What were you always good at? What are some characteristics of you as a child that you still have today? Are there any that have changed? Why did they change?

In the many workshops I've done, there are often people who, when they realize their purpose, realize it's been with them all along. A sudden recognition that, "I knew it! When I was young. I was always performing for people" or "Other kids always came to me with their problems." We are born glowing with innocence. We radiate our gifts as our natural essences. As we get older, we stifle ourselves. We begin to create armor to protect and hide from the world. Take a good look at who you were as a child. You may be surprised how many clues you find there regarding who you want to be today.

Exploring Joy

The next step in finding your purpose is exploring what brings you joy. Think of times you felt extremely happy in your life. What were you doing? What really pumps you up? What are you really passionate about? What would you do even if you had so much money you didn't have to work?

> *Your joy is a pathway that can lead directly to your purpose.*

Joy goes beyond happiness. Happiness and pleasure can be transitory, resulting from changing moods and outer circumstances. Joy springs from deep within the soul when we are expressing our authentic selves—our purposes. When we are on purpose, our life is filled with joy. Accordingly, when we are filled with joy, our life is on purpose.

Don't hold yourself back from what makes you truly joyful. Stifling your joy is surely a slow death.

Remember who you are

Finding purpose is about realizing your own unique connection with the Divine. There is a reason you came down here on this planet. We are all manifestations of the Divine Energy. You may call it God, Jesus, Buddha nature, Allah, Love, the Universe, a Higher Power, or anything you like. Whatever you choose to name it, its creative energy encompasses the entire planet. Everything and everywhere. You are a part of that Divine energy, and your life is a part of that blessing. All of us are the Divine manifested in physical form. We are here as vessels of beautiful love and carry it to all that are around us.

"You are, have always been, and will always be, a *divine part* of the *divine whole*, a *member of the body*," writes Neale Donald Walsch in *Conversations with God*. "That is why the act of rejoining the whole, of returning to God, is called *remembrance*. You actually choose to re-member Who You Really Are."

Your path is unique

However you live your purpose, it will be unique to you. Find your own path, and don't try to imitate others because you think they are more skilled or noble in their purpose.

I was in awe of the monks in Thailand. Abandoning any plan to marry or have children, to acquire money or status, choosing to live a radically simple life, they had come to the monastery to meditate and pray for all beings in the world. Their beneficial energy is changing the world. Just as water is acted upon by positive and negative human words and intentions, so do the monks' prayers and meditations elevate human and planetary strength.

As much as I admired and wanted to be like the monks, I knew that their lifestyle was not my path. I could visit a monastery to get re-fueled, but I knew I wanted to be in the world—in the belly of the beast, helping people wake up. My purpose is to be a lifeguard on the beach of life. I want to help others surf life's waves, ride life's ups and downs, and thrive in the sturm und drang—the storms and stress—of life. I want to administer first aid when others are injured, offer others a hand to grasp when they fear drowning, and cheer them on when they're surfing fine on their own. This is why I became a therapist and life coach.

Sometimes novice monks discover the monastery life is not

their true path. They go through a ceremony called disrobing, and go back out into the world to continue their searching. The other monks always respect this choice, and never try to convince anyone that there is only "one way" to live with purpose. If you find yourself on a path that isn't true, there is no shame in changing your mind and righting your course.

Says the poet Rumi:

> *But don't be satisfied with stories, how things*
> *have gone with others. Unfold*
> *your own myth, without complicated explanation,*
> *so everyone will understand the passage,*
>
> *"We have opened you."*
> *Start walking toward Shams. Your legs will get heavy*
> *and tired. Then comes a moment*
> *of feeling the wings you've grown,*
> *lifting.*

With every step, we walk in love. We are God's messengers and the purpose you are discovering is your Divine message. You may deliver that message to children, adults, or even in corporate America. The poet David Whyte gives brilliant speeches and seminars to corporate clients to help them bring their passionate, creative souls into the workplace through the lessons of poetry and story.

You were born to make apparent the Divinity that is within you and share it with others. This is who you are. There is a beautiful quote by Marianne Williamson in her book, *Return to*

Love, that expresses the essence of our purpose here. I have kept this quote framed in my office for years. It is a constant inspiration to me:

Our deepest fear is not that we are inadequate.
Our deepest fear is we are powerful beyond measure.
It is our light, not our darkness that frightens us.
We ask ourselves, "Who am I to be powerful, glamorous, beautiful, fabulous?"
Who are you NOT to be.

You are a child of God. Your playing small does not serve the world.
We are born to make manifest the glory of God that is within us.
It is not just in some of us, it's in everyone.
And as we let our own light shine, we unconsciously give others permission to do the same.
As we are liberated from our own fear,
Our presence liberates others.

Wake up to your purpose. It is the most important thing you will ever do. Knowledge of your purpose will give joy and hope to your life no matter what happens in your outer world. It is the real reason you are here.

What is your highest purpose? What if you had no excuses, no reasons for not doing it?

Why aren't you doing it now?

—————————————————— **Chapter 7**

Everything is Fuel
Living in Love

Journal Entry

This morning I went on my first alms rounds. Up before dawn, I saw shadows of monks walking toward the Sala with slow, graceful steps. There is a stillness in them, and they are an intrinsic part of the pre-dawn tranquility. They form a line and I fall in at the end, walking toward the villages. The monks are barefoot and carry bowls that will hold the donated food. Their only sustenance. Mine, too. While I am here at Wat Pah Nanachat, I also live on alms food. Alms food. The villagers, who have so little themselves, value sacrificial surrender so much that they share the little food they have with the monks; the food makes up the one meal a day the monks, and guests like me, eat.

The sun rises as we approach the first village. I have my sandals on. My feet are too tender to go barefoot for this long walk. In the village, there are women lined up on the road in front of their impoverished homes. They are barefoot and kneeling. As the monks approach, they bow humbly and put food in the monks' bowls. The monks bow their heads in gratitude as they receive these gifts.

We continue, visiting village after village. All are lined with men, women, and children barefoot and on their knees. The bowls fill. Later, this food will be prepared for the entire monastery and made into the morning meal. The end result is an amazing feast. Beautiful to look at and beautiful to taste. Especially for this spoiled American girl.

Before each meal we chant, "Wisely reflecting, I use alms food: not for fun, not for pleasure, not for fattening, not for beautification, only for the maintenance and nourishment of this body, for keeping it healthy, for helping with the Holy Life. Thinking thus, I will allay hunger without overeating, so that I may continue to live blamelessly and at ease."

My relationship with food has been the total opposite of all we chant. Hunger...beautification...pleasure. PLEASURE! Oh my God. What else is there? It's such pleasure....Italian food, Chinese food, Thai food. I remember my meal at the monastery yesterday. I enjoyed every bite. Eating it was **definitely** a pleasure. But still I chant. In fact, I chant at the top of my starving lungs, hoping some of the wisdom in the words will soak into my brainwashed head.

That night, I struggled with my meditation practice again.

My mind was restless. I opened my eyes and thought, "This just isn't working. I can't concentrate tonight. I should just go to bed." Then I remembered the faces of the villagers kneeling—kneeling!—in front of their homes on the alms rounds. I realized what I should have known all along. **I am doing this for them. I am them.** I must keep going.

What does it mean to love? Is it an act of kindness to a stranger? Your smiling gaze as you talk to a friend? A gentle touch for a lover? Your devotion to your child? However you define love, there is no stronger force on the planet.

"Love is a sacred reserve of energy," said Teilhard de Chardin. "It is like the blood of spiritual evolution."

Nothing in the world is real except love and loving. Moods and emotions aren't real—they are clouds drifting across the sky, changing with each new horizon. Only love is real. Love is the energy that envelopes and permeates the entire planet, the entire universe.

In other cultures there are several words to describe the nuances and types of love. In English we really only have one. It's so limiting to simply use one word, and so confusing! How does this person feel about me? Does he love me like a brother or sister, like a friend, or does he want to take me out on a date? The confusion between the types of love continues to baffle and perplex people.

In the Latin and Greek languages, four words differentiate the types of love we experience in our world: Eros, Philos, Pia, and Agape.

Eros

Eros is romantic or sensual love. It is the love we first feel when the sparks fly between us and another person. It is a feeling of walking on clouds. It is staying up until three in the morning talking or making love, not feeling tired the next day, and wanting to do it all over again. When you experience Eros, you find yourself thinking about the other person frequently. They seem perfect for you—problems are non-existent, or at least solvable. Eros is the magic love that songs are written about and movies help us revisit, again and again.

There is a dark side to the magic of Eros, as well. Erotic love can be controlling and possessive. Erotic love can be filled with criteria, expectation, protection, and constriction. How can you protect me from my own insecurities? How can you save me from my fear? We want to have an endless supply of good feelings, and we don't want to share this person with anyone else. We may try to restrict the other person's life in order to alleviate our own pain or fear. We are afraid to live without this person, and so we grasp them tighter and tighter.

The dark side of Eros has ruined so many relationships. When the grip of one person in the relationship becomes too tight, the other stops being true to who they are. Hobbies and outside interests are abandoned, communication with friends becomes minimal, and soon what was once beautiful and enlarging becomes a prison. Then the anger and jealousy begin.

Erotic love must transform in order to become lasting, deep, and true. Without Eros, we might never initially be attracted to one another, and without its metamorphosis, we will never stay together.

Philos

Philos, like its namesake Philadelphia, is the "city of brotherly love." Sometimes called platonic love, it is the love of friendship, of a child, a brother or sister, a teacher or mentor. Philos is pure and powerful. Without judgment. The gift of Philos is its ability to inspire and empower us. When someone loves us in this way, we begin to feel confident and motivated, comforted or nurtured.

Philos love keeps us from feeling alone in a scary world. It creates the spirit of union with all things and beings. This love reminds us that we are part of something much greater than ourselves. You can express a Philos love for animals, people, nature, and even places that inspire you.

Pia

Pia is a familial love, the kind of love a parent feels for his or her child. Pia is one of the most powerful bonds in nature and is expressed in animal as well as human societies. This love often leads to self-sacrifice for the sake of the family and children.

Agape

Agape is a transcendent love that flows from the spirit. Agape is loving without attachment or conditions. Without anxiety about what's in it for you, or about the future. It is loving for the sake of loving. Loving without fear. Or feeling the fear and loving big anyway. Agape is fearless loving.

Agape has also been called unconditional love. When you love in this way, no one has to prove him or herself to you. The other person is accepted as who they are—you have no need to change them to fit your mold or protect you from fear. Sometimes loving big even means letting go. It means loving yourself big enough and trusting your life enough that you don't need to hold on to what is not working.

Agape is a re-enactment of God's love on earth. It is being a foundation for other people so they can be nurtured and inspired to their highest selves. Even at the cost of suffering for you.

We have all felt the pain of an important relationship's end. Agape Love means letting go with grace and knowing that the universe is working exactly as it should.

It doesn't mean not feeling pain, but opening fully, feeling fully, and letting go fully. This poem by Mary Oliver has always struck me as the essence of Agape love:

To live in this world you must be able to do three things,
To love what is mortal,
To hold it against your bones knowing your own life depends on it,
And when it comes time to let it go, to let it go.

Agape is a heart-filled, glorious love that you feel right down to your core.

All the Loves in Life

The happiest and most long-lasting marriages and unions are the ones that flow through all the stages of love. Eros inspires their initial attraction. Then as they get to truly know each other, Philos grows between them. We've all heard happy couples declare that they are each other's best friend. If they have children, Pia will enter their union as well. Finally, as they come to accept and love the other person unconditionally, Agape creates enduring joy and light.

Agape love can be given freely to any being and to any thing. It is the recognition that life is a dazzling, interwoven web of existence. You are not outside, looking in. You are a part of all that exists—human, animal, vegetable and mineral— from the atoms of your body to the Divine essence of your soul.

Many daily practices can lead you to Agape.

Love for oneself

Loving oneself is the only way to give big love. Without self-love, you are trying to give while standing on unstable ground—always worried about falling, losing your balance, or hurting yourself. We've all heard it before—you can't love anyone else unless you truly love yourself. That means you have to be strong enough in yourself to love without fear of outcome.

The biggest obstacle to loving oneself is ingrained faulty belief systems such as *I am not OK, I am not enough, I don't trust God or life,* or *I am not worthy.* Self-love expands when you practice your new truths rather than these old, erroneous beliefs.

Who is reinforcing those beliefs now? After all these years, you may be the one still putting yourself through the ringer of self-defeat. Love for oneself means forgiving yourself for all the ways you have judged yourself over the years. Healing yourself of these belief systems means going inside, seeing yourself as the child you were, feeling the feelings of old, and yet having compassion for the amazing being that you are. This is the bounty of unconditional love for yourself.

Small, conditional love is easy. Small love can create lots of verbal "I love yous" while really meaning, "I love you as long as you do what I say, fulfill my needs, and meet my expectations."

Big Agape love comes from a place of fullness and expansion, not emptiness needing to be filled. It honors the other person and their choices even if you don't fully agree. It embraces the other person, and wishes them well, even as they are walking away from you.

The only way to truly experience big love is to trust your life and your path. When you have this ultimate trust in yourself, you know everything is manifesting perfectly as your life unfolds. Even if it doesn't make sense at the time.

When you love yourself, you stand unafraid with no need to protect or defend. No matter what anyone else says or thinks about you. You are able to meet all people with a gentle smile, whatever their opinions or beliefs. Nothing threatens who you are inside. Truly loving oneself is the ultimate freedom, the ultimate impenetrable strength.

Find compassion for yourself. Most of us are harder on ourselves than we are on our worst enemies. Recognize and release those internal voices that say horrible things about you. Don't beat yourself up. Many of us remember the words from Max Ehrmann's Desiderata:

Beyond a wholesome discipline,
be gentle with yourself.
You are a child of the universe,

no less than the trees and the stars;
you have a right to be here.
And whether or not it is clear to you,
no doubt the universe is unfolding as it should.

You help create your life with words and beliefs. Don't treat yourself badly. You are worthy of gentleness and compassion.

Simple Kindness

Kindness starts by treating others with respect, and listening to them from your heart. What an impact it would have on society if we treated everyone like they were the most important person in the world. They are important. Everyone and everything has something to teach you.

Kindness is the Golden Rule taught by all religions—to treat others as you yourself wish to be treated. Here is a portion of the Buddha's words on kindness from the Metta Sutra.

So with a boundless heart
Should one cherish all living beings:
Radiating kindness over the entire world
Spreading upwards to the skies,
And downwards to the depths;
Outwards and unbounded...

There are times when a smile or word of encouragement can pull someone back from the brink. Simple and random acts of kindness can change your life. An energetic ripple effect sends love radiating out around you and back to you.

Joy

You can choose to experience joy rather than misery in any situation. Joy requires that you be in the present moment, with thoughts unclouded by future or past. Even in the midst of pain and difficulty, the most mundane situations contain a spark of humor and joy. Inhale the brisk pine-scented air as you shovel snow off the sidewalk. Feel the warm summer sun on your face as you weed the garden. Dance in the rain. Realize the miracle of your heartbeat, your breath, your footsteps as you walk your dog.

Smile. Even when you don't feel like it. Scientific research has shown that our attitudes and feelings will come to match our physical body posture. Simply standing straight and erect can make you feel more confident. Smiling can make you feel happy. If you are not joyful right now, smile and pretend to be. Soon you will be. Thicht Nhat Hanh calls smiling "yoga for the mouth."

Celebrate life. Your joy will naturally radiate out to others, giving them a gift of laughter and light.

Choose your activities wisely and seek the joy in each event. Don't blame others if you have too much work to do, and you are running around like a crazy person from commitment to commitment and "must-do" tasks. The job you keep working at, the people around you, even the way you spend your leisure time are your choices. Choose consciously, and then don't blame anyone else for creating your reality. Saying "yes" when we mean "no" is one of the most damaging things we can do to ourselves. Doing anything purely out of a sense of obligation or a need to please other people is a surefire way to create resentment and kill your joy.

Before you agree to any activity, take the time to listen to yourself. It's okay to say to another person, "Hold on a sec, I have to think about that." During that time take a deep breath. Ask yourself, do I really want to do this activity or task? Will this create joy in my life? If the answer is yes, commit to it fully and joyfully. If the answer is no, be very careful about agreeing to participate in the project or activity.

Living in joy means using every opportunity that life gives you as an opportunity for growth. When I work with athletes we have a saying, "Use everything as fuel." That means finding the lesson, the meaningfulness, in every situation. Even if the situation seems negative on the surface, there is a positive message hidden. Every moment is an opportunity to learn and move forward. Ask yourself, what is the good here? How can I take this moment and derive joy from it? Where is my life lesson that will make me stronger, wiser, more compassionate? Finding the gift of every moment is the key to discovering the beauty that surrounds you at all times.

Your joy is a seed inside you, waiting to bloom. Nourish it. Trust it. Encourage it.

Compassion

Even a small amount of compassion can change the world's energy. Compassion is empathy—the opening of your heart to the suffering you see. It does not mean constantly running to rescue and save everyone you meet. Running around rescuing is simply a reinforcement of the belief system that cries out, *I am only loved when I save others.* You are worth so much more than that. When you show compassion, you express nonjudgmental Agape love both verbally and non-verbally.

Every person is simply trying to make it work down here in our crazy world. We're all doing our best to be happy, and find a place with minimal pain. We are all interconnected. Your joy and suffering are someone else's joy and suffering.

The three kinds of Pride spoken of in Buddhism are: 1) thinking I am better than others, 2) thinking I am worse than others, and 3) thinking I am just as good as others. In other words, there are no "others." We are all a spark of the same Divine essence.

When you begin to judge and label another person, you are automatically responding from pride and a desire to make them "other" than you. We may say, "Why does she stay with that abusive jerk?" or "I can't believe he did that to me!" If you stop to reflect on how you would behave under the same circumstances, you may gain a little empathy. Let yourself feel their pain and confusion, the fear that haunts them. Then practice opening your heart. Understand the struggle of all people to find comfort in their lives. To feel safety and love. The struggles of one are the struggles of the many. We are all in the same boat.

When you judge another, it often arises from your own past hurts and disappointments, from fear or insecurities, from the need to be right. Examine your own heart and mind to become aware of the root of your judgment. Ask yourself, "What in me needs to heal? How can I nurture myself? How can I forgive myself for my self-judgments and have compassion?"

Compassion means understanding and loving even when you don't agree with another's behavior, decision, or point of view. It does not mean giving up your values or giving in to another person when you don't agree. It's simply a state of honoring another for his or her process and trusting that the process will unfold exactly as it is meant to.

When I saw the old monk in Nepal, gently moving earthworms one by one to safety after a rain, tears sprang to my eyes at his amazing compassion. How many earthworms had I stepped on that day already? What if people were earthworms? How many "earthworms" do I step on every day? I thought how wonderful life would be if we treated everyone with as much care as he did these humble creatures, lifting our fellow beings to their own sense of safety.

All energy is interconnected. Practice compassion for all things, be it a bug on the ground, a plant, or even the vacuum cleaner you want to kick. Save a spider, notice what is under your feet when you walk, plant flowers, and leave the air conditioning on for your dog. Any kindness sent into the world is kindness drawn back toward you.

Tonglen is a Buddhist practice that means sending and taking. No matter what your religious or spiritual beliefs are, this practice is a great way to open your heart to compassion. Tonglen is a powerful practice and requires a little courage. If you do it consistently, you will find over time that your shields and armor begin to slip away, revealing the essence of you—a warm heart softened by empathy and love, a heart expanded by the courage, openness and compassion of the spiritual warrior.

You can do this practice as a meditation or prayer, or you can do it in the moment whenever you see someone is in need of help or healing. Begin by concentrating on the in-and-out of your breathing. On the in-breath, open your heart to someone else's pain and suffering. Let yourself feel the pain of another being, of humanity or the world in general. Suffering is part of human existence and you will not close yourself off to it.

On the out-breath, exhale all the peace, fearlessness, joy, love, and faith you have ever felt outwards to the source of the suffering.

In the practice of Tonglen, says Pema Chodron, "you actually invite in not only all your own unresolved conflicts, confusion, and pain, but also those of other people. And it goes even further....not only are we willing to breathe in painful things, we are also willing to breathe out our feelings of well-being, peace, and joy. We are willing to give these away, to share them with others."

Chodron states that you can do Tonglen if you have ever had even one moment of suffering or one moment of happiness in your life. Practice breathing Tonglen whenever you see someone in need. Breathe in their suffering or pain. Breathe out and wish them happiness and peace.

Practice Tonglen on someone who needs it this week. It could be a homeless person on the street, your co-worker going through a divorce, or a traffic accident you see on the freeway. Simply begin the sending and taking process. Do Tonglen for those who are starving, suffering in prison, or at war. Do Tonglen for yourself. Do Tonglen for other forms of life as well: a tree being cut down, animals at the humane society, or the bugs smashed on your windshield are a good start.

Gratitude

Gratitude is a practice that can melt away fear, worry, and armor like no other. Gratitude is more than just saying "Thank you." Gratitude is a way of life, an energy that is pervasive throughout your entire being. Like love, Gratitude can be looked at as either something you do, or a state of being, or both.

We have all had experiences for which we feel grateful. A job promotion, a success, a close call avoided, a friend who comes to our aid. Remember how you felt in your body and heart at such times. In times of gratitude we are closest to God—closest to feeling the love that we were meant to feel as we go through our everyday lives.

"If the only prayer you said in your whole life was, 'Thank you,' that would suffice," said Meister Eckhart. The best prayer, writes Neale Donald Walsh, is "never a prayer of supplication, but a prayer of gratitude."

Living in gratitude means looking at life through the eyes of a child and seeing with wonder all the marvelous things in this world. It is appreciating all that life has to offer—the joys and the sorrows, the times you want to jump for joy and the times you want to collapse in pain.

Gratitude is a celebration of life itself.

Look at your life. Marvel at how awesome it is. The miracle of your body. How, day in and day out, it supports you and carries you through your life. Notice the wonder of nature: plants, animals, insects, and the incredible nature of the Earth itself. There is so much to be grateful for every day. The people in your life, the friends who brought you joy, and the ones that taught you painful lessons. Know that your life is an amazing puzzle, where friend and foe have beautifully orchestrated their place in it to bring you to this moment.

Today, take nothing for granted. Imagine what the world would be like without your car, the heat or air conditioning in your house, or the flowers that line your walkway. Take a moment to notice things you generally take for granted. Give silent thanks for all the things they bring to you.

When I was eating the alms food donated by the Thai people, I felt grateful for every bite. The villagers had little, yet daily they donated some of their meager food as an offering to others.

What if you had one day to live? How would you see the world differently? What if you lost your eyesight tomorrow? What are the things you would miss? How would you see the world differently if it were your last day to see? Living in gratitude means recognizing that nothing is permanent. Everything is a gift that could be taken away tomorrow.

Have you ever injured a small part of your body and noticed what a big effect it had on your entire day? I broke my toe when I was a child involved in gymnastics. It was my baby toe, a toe I thought did very little to affect my life. As I limped around, pain shooting up my leg, I realized just how important this "insignificant" part of my body was! My entire balance was off for weeks. I had a new appreciation for the "little" things when I healed fully.

If you have ever had to recover from an illness or accident, I'm sure life felt fresh and new when you were yourself again. You were grateful just to be able to walk again without pain, or breathe easily, or use your arms or hands.

When we live in gratitude, our joy spills over on others. We celebrate others' successes as we do our own. This is Gratitude with a capital "G." Not simply being thankful for circumstances that serve you and your ego, but "sympathetic gratitude" for all others.

A gratitude contemplation

This is a simple gratitude contemplation that you can do every day of the week. Spend ten minutes a day and contemplate any of the following reasons for gratitude.

To begin, find a quiet room in your house that is private and relaxing. Sit in a comfortable position and begin to slowly and gently focus on your breathing. Let your breaths be natural, in and out, without control or force. Simply allow yourself to relax naturally and follow your breath. Focus your attention on your heart. Gently see your breath massaging and opening your heart. Imagine your breath swirling around your heart, moving with each beat, opening and massaging more and more. Feel a sense of peace within your body.

Day One:

As your breath flows throughout your body, imagine it easing away tension, soothing aches and pains, providing healing wherever it is necessary. Give blessings to your entire body. Thank all your organs and cells for their endless service. Pay special attention to the parts that have struggled or suffered through pain or illness. Bathe your body, your senses, and all of your cells, in gratitude.

Day Two:

Practice gratitude for your loved ones and friends. Remember how much they have given you. How they nurture you every day. Place each of them before you in your imagination. Send them love, peace, and gratitude.

Day Three

Experience gratitude for the Earth and all the Earth's beings. Give thanks for the trees that provide you oxygen to breathe. The oceans with their majesty and power. And all the Earth's creatures that provide you with food and friendship. Be grateful for the flowers with their beauty. The mountains offering their watchful eye. Have gratitude for all the Earth provides you every day.

Day Four

Offer gratitude to all of your teachers. Who are the teachers and mentors that have influenced your life? It may be schoolteachers, or coaches, parents, or people involved in your church. Give thanks for all of those teachers. Now, give thanks to other teachers in your life, those that taught you the "hard" lessons of fear or heartbreak. Thank them for the lessons they have taught you that impacted you so much.

Day Five

Practice gratitude for all the suffering you have encountered in your life. It might be physical suffering or emotional suffering. It might have been caused by others or by yourself. This is a difficult practice, so be patient with yourself. Imagine all the suffering you have experienced, and thank it for the lessons it has taught you. Acknowledge that without the knowledge, pain, and growth from these experiences, you would not be who you are today.

Day Six

Today, sit in gratitude for your amazing life. Give thanks to God or whomever you view as Universal Energy. Thank this life for the opportunity to live, be, and experience all of its joys and sorrows. Thank God for all the gifts you have received and the ability to pass these gifts on to others.

Day Seven

Practice gratitude for yourself. Imagine yourself standing before you. Tell yourself how proud you are to know you. Thank yourself for the gifts you have given to the world. For your courage and strength, and for the kindness you have shown to others. Forgive yourself of any wrongdoings or guilt. Shower yourself with love and gratitude.

Reverence

The traditional Buddhist greeting is "Namaste." Namaste means, "The God essence in me, bows and honors the God essence in you." With reverence, we live a life that acknowledges the divinity in all things. All creatures and all humans—all of existence—are sacred.

When I was first exposed to this concept, I became conscious of walking across a blade of grass. How many times had I just stomped across, without noticing? How many times had I plucked a flower or the leaf of a tree in mindless distraction? Reverence is awareness of the alive-ness of everything. Honoring all of life. That doesn't mean that you never pick a flower. What it does mean is that you *notice* when you are picking a flower and honor the beauty and sacrifice of that living thing. What a wonderful way to live! When you are reverent, you value life. You value the farmer that grew the food on your dinner table tonight. You value the animal that gave its life so you could be nourished.

Live today with reverence for all living things. Every living being on this planet has value. Every thing we view as "non-living" is made up of moving atoms. Does this not make it alive as well? Reverence is a way of living. Take nothing for granted.

Love as a state of being

Living "in love" means actually living fully in the present. When one is truly in the present, all there is to see is love. Being in love is opening your heart fully to what is in every moment. Remember the "being present with someone you love" meditation in Chapter Three? What if you interacted with the entire Universe from that place of being? If you did, you would find yourself falling into love with an abundance of people, trees, experiences, and moments!

You can live in a state of love. You can be love in every moment. Are you in love right now?

We sometimes talk of "falling in love" as if it is something that happens *to* us—a wondrous event that is completely out of our control. Yet falling in love can be a conscious choice—a life filled with love is entirely within your power to create.

You can create within your heart an expansive love for people, animals, mountains, plants, for all of creation in its mystery and wonder. You can fall in love with life itself, and seduce it into revealing its secrets and joys.

When you are in love there is an opening of your heart to whatever is in the moment. Without criticism of a person or situation. There is surrender into the knowing that each moment is part of the Divine. Each moment is perfect. Whenever I sit and breathe consciously and look into the eyes of another person, I fall in love with them. Falling in love with someone doesn't mean you want to sleep with him or her or even want to hold them close. Falling in love is a big, grand, beautiful, embracing Agape love—an unconditional flow of caring and recognition.

When you fall in love this way, your love is not conditioned on someone else's response to you. People who have been hurt can sometimes respond cynically to love—wondering what you want from them, what's your angle, fearing you'll get too close. Yet expressions of love need no response. It's like that "Butterfly in the Hand." You cherish its presence and its beauty, but you never try to close your hand around it.

Imagine love as a container of energy. That energy surrounds you. You only need to surrender to it. The fact is, you are in it now. You are it. You are a fish and love is the ocean. Not only do you swim in it, you are also composed of it entirely. Being in love is walking day-in-day-out with kindness, joy, compassion, gratitude, reverence and understanding. You control, simply by being present, the amount of love in your life. Jealousy, protectiveness, blame, and fear are the biggest obstacles to love. Let go of what holds you back from living in a state of love. To live in a state of love is heaven on this earth.

Dedicate your life as a monument to the Divine. Love is the greatest force on the planet. Every cell of your body is composed of it. Do you really think you are this personality? One of the most powerful meditations I practice is the mantra, *I am not this body.* When I remind myself of this truth over and over, I can disconnect from the personality of Alison and truly embrace myself as a part of the Divine.

When you truly discover who you are, you find there is no YOU after all.

When you walk through your life in a state of love everything is effortless. You don't even have to try to make things happen, they simply happen. Take a deep breath now. Open your heart. Walk through this day as if you are Love embodied. Walk with a smile, with reverence for all people and their struggles. Walk through this day as if you are Love embodied. You are Love's puppet. Walk with a smile, with reverence for all people and their struggles. Are you in love right now? Choose to create it.

Inside this new love, die.
Your way begins on the other side.
Become the sky.
Take an ax to the prison wall.
Escape.
Walk out like someone suddenly born into color.
Do it now.
—*Rumi*

Devouring the Dark Mother

Journal Entry 12/4/01

I'm back home. When my plane landed in Phoenix, I was nearly bursting with joy. I was so happy. I felt so open and alive. Every cell in my being exuded love for family and friends.

So many reactions from people when they hear about my pilgrimage. Curiosity, interest, horror that I would even think of sleeping on the forest floor with the ants. My boss at USA Gymnastics was relieved that I hadn't shaved my head. She was afraid I would scare the athletes!

Maybe some of my neuroses and selfishness did die somewhere along the journey. But now, two weeks later, chaos has descended. Appointments have needed to be changed. My schedule is busy, demanding, rushed. Our office was robbed. Bills are due. My laptop crashed. I feel angry and hard, as if I want to erect a shield against the world again. Put back on the armor. It's as if the Universe is saying to me, "So you thought you were different. HA! Here is reality—deal with it." What a test it is.

It is easy to be loving when you are a monk on a mountain top. But can I, can we, continue to wake up and love in the belly of the beast—in the rush and trials of our daily lives? I realize my journey is only the beginning. Now is the true test. To continue to die to the "I" so I can live and give fully in every moment. To discard my protective coats as quickly as I reach for them, and open my naked heart to the world. To scream my truth without falling prey to the old pattern-silencers. I know Nepal and Thailand helped me—I've melted my armor, even if only a little. My travels have helped me to find my purpose. I identify with the Dalai Lama's favorite quote, by the Buddhist saint Shantideva:

> For as long as space endures,
> and for as long as living beings remain,
> until then may I too abide
> to dispel the misery of the world.

I know that I was born to help alleviate the suffering of all beings. We are all born to do this holy mission. Whether we are a teacher, parent, coach, mortgage broker, salesperson. This is what dying to self is all about. This is what it is to recognize our Divine interconnectedness, our dependence and need for each other. "Driven by the forces of love, the fragments of the world seek each other so that the world may come to being," wrote Teilhard de Chardin.

So today, amidst the chaos, e-mails, insurance claims, and traffic, I vow to live awake and with love. I know I can't be perfect every day. But I can be as fully alive in each moment as I choose to be. ⁓

Whenever I sat down to do a meditation in Thailand or Nepal—which was as often as five times a day—I would always recite two poems in addition to the traditional Buddhist blessings. The first is a poem by Rumi, which I regard as a sacred prayer. The poem is a call, an incantation to love. For me it was a pleading—may love bless me enough to open me, flow through me, and allow me to be it's humble servant.

It is a powerful prayer with which to begin your day or any meditation:

Oh love, O pure deep love, be here, be now, Be all.

Worlds dissolve into your stainless endless radiance,

Frail living leaves burn with you brighter than cold stars,

Make me your servant, your breath, your core.

The second prayer I said was a version of what has become known as the Peace Prayer of Saint Francis:

Lord, help me to be an instrument of thy peace.

Where there is hatred, let me sow love.

Where there is injury, pardon

Where there is doubt, faith

Where there is despair, hope

Where there is darkness, light

Where there is sadness, joy.

Lord, grant me that I may not so much seek,

To be consoled, as to console,

To be understood, as to understand,

To be loved, as to love.

For it is in giving that we receive

It is in pardoning that we are pardoned

It is in dying to self that we are re-born into everlasting life.

In Nepal and Thailand, I wanted to learn to die to my old life and my old neurotic self—to be born again into a new Love and a new Life. I'm still learning. Still understanding that I am so much more than this body and this personality.

In my mind's eye, I see the cremation of the young girl who died of AIDS, remembering her body as it lay with all her belongings on woodpiles that crackled from the heat of the dancing fire. As I watched her body burn, piece by piece, I continued to chant as the Monks instructed, "This is my body. This is my skin, this is my hair, this is my heart." There was a moment I felt her presence with me, knew that she was not this body and in that exact instant I had a clarity that shattered all of my physical senses. I am not this body. In that moment all of my neurosis—my work, my life, my self-importance burned like her ashes, spiraling into the wind.

This is such an amazing, crazy Life. It is my hope that this book has helped you awaken into the wonderful Life that is yours. Our time here is so short and so precious. We must devour every minute, every situation. Life is not something to shield yourself from—it is something to run toward, to fling yourself into Life's arms and let it flood over you and flow through every cell in your body. Can you do it? Can you live so fearlessly that in every event and every situation you open yourself to Life rather than closing yourself off?

I met someone recently who told me how he chose to live after being diagnosed with brain cancer. "I *eat* everything life brings to me," he said. "Devour it with joy. I found joy when my lover died of AIDS, I found joy in my brain tumor. Whatever the dark mother brings to me...I breathe it in and devour it hungrily."

Who is the "dark mother?" In Hindu tradition, she is Kali— a fearful, dark goddess with a mother's heart. Kali is both a loving, protecting mother and a destroyer. To me, she represents death and rebirth, the often painful death of ego so that all can become new, again and again.

The world ebbs and flows in a complete circle of destruction and creation. We cannot eliminate pain, sorrow, death, and destruction in this life. They have important lessons to teach us. Kali's gift is freedom—the freedom and fearlessness that emerge when we confront suffering and death and learn to revel in the moment, to devour every precious moment that Life grants us, to celebrate it all—to embrace even the Dark Mother. To breathe in the joy and pain of this life. Cry and wail with reckless abandon. Cackle and laugh at the top of your lungs.

To accept your pain and mortality is to be able to let go, to begin to sing, dance, and shout. To breathe out all the joy, love, laughter, compassion, amazement and wonder that is in your soul. Don't resist the siren call. Just give it up. Surrender to Life, surrender to Love. Let Life and Love flow through your heart, your mind, your blood, every cell in your body, your very being.

This book is the beginning of a journey that never ends. Now that you've gotten to the end, it's time to go back to the beginning. This is the way of all spiritual practice. Awakening is not a linear process—it's the circular climb of an upward arching spiral. Each end flows into a new beginning. Peace becomes chaos, then peace again. Each death is a rebirth. We sleep and wake to an eternal rhythm.

Keep waking up. Keep surrendering. Keep opening. Are you ready to Scream and Run Naked?

The Beginning

Want to Scream and Run Naked?

Continue to explore who you are and what you want to create with Alison's new workbook, *Living the Scream and Run Naked Life: Uncovering Your Authentic Presence.* This fourteen-week journal and practice helps you unwrap the blockages that keep you stuck and re-awakens your authenticity and fire. Seize the power in your life by changing old beliefs and becoming the person you were meant to be.

Immerse yourself in the Scream and Run Naked Experience!

Visit www.screamandrunnaked.com to learn more about amazing weekend workshops and other seminars.

What they are saying about
Scream and Run Naked workshops....

Alison's workshops were inspiring, thought provoking and got our staff living the Scream and Run Naked Life. Not only are they happier, but our sales went up 20%! **—Russ Perlich, President, of Quadna**

I didn't think it could happen, but I'm leaving this weekend a different person. I feel awake, and alive in ways I never thought possible. I know I am in control of my life and everything that happens to me. I'm not waiting for my life to begin any more! **—KW, Gilbert, AZ**

www.screamandrunnaked.com
www.headgames.ws

Printed in the United States
68297LVS00003B/145-252